BASKETBALL PLAYS, TRICKS AND GIMMICKS

BASKETBALL PLAYS, TRICKS AND GIMMICKS

Wm. J. Coste

1999 NATIONAL HIGH SCHOOL
COACH OF THE YEAR
JULY 10, 2010

Library of Congress Control Number:		2010911597
ISBN:	Hardcover	978-1-4535-5340-4
	Softcover	978-1-4535-5339-8
	Ebook	978-1-4535-5341-1

This book was printed in the United States of America.

To order additional copies of this book, contact:
Xlibris Corporation
1-888-795-4274
www.Xlibris.com
Orders@Xlibris.com
83918

Contents

Foreword

My first exposure to basketball was at a high school game in Bothell, Washington. I didn't take to it immediately. I was in the first grade. A first grader's initial focus at a basketball game is the gym's bleachers and what they had to offer for climbing on. However, minutes into the pregame warm-ups, my eyes become riveted on the game not because of its action or colorful uniforms but because of one Bothell High School player. He captivated my attention. My interest was fascinated with this player because of the lack of an ear—an unfortunate early childhood accident caused by the explosion of an oil stove. He was an all-league player. Fortunate for me because at first, that is not what won my attention. I suppose for a five—or six-year-old, the exposed hole in the side of another one's head would be unashamedly alluring and natural to fixate on. My full undivided attention of his malady was the indirect cause of my acquaintance with basketball. It wasn't until later in the game that I took notice of his extraordinary basketball talents in comparison to the other players. The game became mysteriously fun to watch. I became hooked. Thank you Bothell mystery guard, wherever you are. You changed my life.

My early understanding of this game, which was before Converse All-Stars went to white low cuts, was that it was won by the team that made the most baskets. Seemed simple. Even as a grade school student, I immediately grasped the idea. I thought I did. As I neared high school and began thinking about my future, my interest leaned toward this simple game. I had other sports interests: I was a big Fighting Irish fan and a loyal Yankee fan. Back then, the success of the Irish and the Bronx Bombers made it easy and rewarding to follow them. They won a lot, which made them seem very faithful to me, although my passion was playing hoops and I planned to continue to play it as long as I could. I figured that once my "hops" were gone, I would still continue being a part of the game. Maybe I should coach it. This would permit me to retain an interest so dear and be compensated for it. Perfect! How hard could it be?

I was not naive to the system. I knew that job longevity and pay was going to be connected with my coaching success. Success in high school and college basketball is, by the most part, defined by winning. How could my teams win more than they lost? The answer seemed simple: my teams would outshoot the other teams. So how could I guarantee my team would score more baskets than my opponents? I would coach players to become excellent shooters. I would begin shooting clinics at the grade school for developing those myriad young LeBron copycats. This seemed to be the first logical step necessary for guaranteeing my rise within the coaching ranks. I wondered if all coaches took this route. Too simple—they would all be winning. What was I overlooking? I would still begin with developing hot shooting players. My teams would outscore their opponents.

However, at a basketball clinic, I heard a speaker state that you could assist shooters to become better shooters but you could not develop pure shooters—scorers maybe, but not pure shooters. Many in the audience nodded their heads with reconciliatory moans of agreement much like newly indoctrinated cult members. If the speaker was correct, and I am sure he was by the audience response, my task for success seemed to waver a might. Outscore your opponents not by outshooting them but by stopping them from scoring. An interesting idea: winning by defense? Still a simple game—just outscore your opponent by making more baskets. This idea seemed even simpler than my earlier plan: you didn't even need a ball. Intersperse coaching fierce defense with making better shooters. Surely others have thought this through—how could I make a difference? Tall players would probably help. Very tall players would be better.

I wanted good compensation and job security. I also wanted to be successful and to be loved. The simple game of basketball seemed to be the avenue for my wishes. Unfortunately, no one could give me a concrete formula for generating success by developing those strange defensive priorities with my shooters. And how was I to develop very tall players? That's a genetic thing!

In my early research, I read where many of the greatest coaches in the country attributed outscoring opponents to playing great defense. However, nothing ever seems so simple than it appears to be. While I was in high school, John Wooden was beginning his dynasty and total control of the NCAA basketball program. It appeared simple to attribute somewhat of his coaching success to his players and their offensive skills. Alcindor, Bibby, Allen, Walton, Wicks, Rowe, Wilkes—they toted hall of fame names before they played the game. On and on, his teams were inundated by All-Americans. Then I listened to Coach Wooden talk about his high-post offense, his 221 press, and his carefully formulated Pyramid of Success. And I realized there was much more to his basketball success than the players he recruited. His situation caused my consternation over the argument of the importance of players versus coaches. *Anyone could win with good players? Good players could overcome a bad coach? Which is more important,* I thought, *a good coach or good players?*

If we begin by looking at the players, are we looking at offensive players or defenders? Adding to the confusion of offensive personnel, we hear about shooters and scorers, play makers, finishers, leaders, height and quickness and ball savvy. No simple offensive standard and method of formulating are the same. Players who specialized in defense spoke of defending the dribble, the pass, the shot, the zone. Defensive jargon was completely foreign to me. Defense is not taught on the playgrounds of America. Perry Mason, the television attorney, was adept at nonsustained defensive moves. I understood those defensive actions. Popular girls in my high school probably knew more about defensive moves than I did. The simpleness of finding success in coaching basketball was beginning to elude me. The unified theory of encompassing special relativity with quantum physics is probably more difficult, because no one has figured it out. An ex-German theoretical physics science professor at Princeton was still working on it on his death bed, on his home court.

When evaluating other coaches, my assistant and I used to discuss problems with certain coaches' respective X's & O's or their inability to pass on their thoughts to create what was in their minds, their inability to set a motivating environment or their inability to make able and effectual adjustments, their inability to recruit and to retain players. We recognized those coaches that did have the abilities, but it was hard to understand why. I listen to fellow coaches who have considerable knowledge and understanding of the game's intricacies and wonder over their inability to win games. On the other hand, I listen to other coaches who seem to lack the inner knowledge of the game but continue to succeed. Add in the intangibles of player experience, coaching experience, home game schedules, friendly gyms, injuries, team numbers and/or depth, thigh-high game shorts, and the difficulty in beating a team three times causes wonder. Simple has now become difficult, incomprehensible, and sometimes impossible.

So is there a concrete formula for coaching success? Not to oversimplify, but my experience leans toward a coach who lives for the game and can pass on his knowledge; these coaches have a good start toward success. Add to this coach a team roster of players composed of quick and tall athletes, then you are on the road to the complex answer on how to outscore your opponents. However, all things being equal but quite the opposite, numerous coaches must play with a lesser balanced assembly of personnel. Many coaches must deal with stacked decks, such as teams that have to hide certain players. Some are coaching teams so young that many of their players would have a hard time entering an R-rated movie or they are coaching teams with players too short for riding carnival rides. Unfortunately, to make things worse, these disadvantaged teams do not generate added pay for their coaches. They should, but they don't.

To win with teams lacking in talent or teams who do not dream of miracles is difficult and emotionally draining. A career as a theoretical physics scientist might be more involved and more difficult than coaching basketball, but I wager the scientist sleeps better. Classroom teachers seem to look at their colleagues that are coaching with an inferior perspective because of the time off and for the interruptive trips but most of all because of the importance that students place on their sport. I have often thought that to be the ultimate teacher of a high school classroom, it should be filled with parents and classroom fans. The lessons taught should be reviewed by testing against other schools twice a week. Every other test should be on the road. Those tests should be held in front of the parents and fans. The press should be invited. There should be interviews after the tests with the press so teachers are held accountable for their class scores. They should be shown on television. I'm sure if this expanded, if Socrates' teaching method was adopted by the school districts, that teachers would certainly appreciate more what coaches endure. More important, this "dog and pony" show would probably improve learning and gravitate educators toward sager pedagogical techniques. *Piaget would have to include a new developmental stage.*

It is to be hoped that this book of basketball tricks and gimmicks will somewhat supplement your team deficiencies and help form some helpful steps for your personal success. I have included numerous forms and letters for the neophyte coaches. Hopefully, this will save time and research for those new to coaching basketball. Coaches are always looking for an edge, and when all things are equal, a book of gimmicks and tricks should be inviting. It is also my wish that this book will help guide you and relieve what fears you may have about coaching.

I remember, as a young coach, as I was approaching my first high school contest: Two nights before the game, at a Nike basketball clinic, I thought I overheard coaches mentioning a fake TO. A fake time-out? What was a fake time-out? I did not know. Would I even recognize one if it was used against my team? Was I really ready to coach? Had I prepared my team adequately? I thought I had. Crap! I remember thinking that I would not sleep that night. Does a team hide during a fake time-out? If so, why? As I was entering the gym on the eve of that first contest, still pondering on my readiness, it hit me. A fake TO. *Turnover!* Not a *time-out.* A fake turnover. Talk about a dose of instant catharsis; but what was a fake turnover? I did not know. Was I ready to coach this game? Crap again! Would my players recognize another team's fake turnover? I wondered, *Could my team execute a fake turnover? If so, would they know why?* That night, I think I called out three times for a fake turnover. This order was purely for the crowd's amazement and my opponent's amusement, for I just wanted to appear to be knowledgeable and in control. I think we converted on two, I don't know, that whole contest is now a blur. The third one, which I thought should have iced the game for us, wasn't used. My team captain misunderstood and thought I had called for a fake time-out . . . No, the game is far from outscoring your opponents by making more baskets. It involves using tricks and gimmicks.

Chapter 1

Building a Program

Building a program takes time. It takes enthusiasm and exertion. Your work ethics will be challenged with the connecting of correct personnel with their applicable X's and O's. You should be further encumbered by the challenge of injecting the correct motivational environment. It takes much self-confidence. It takes constant research and self-study. You must have an unwavering mental tenacity for sticking to it. Setbacks occur, but your willingness to learn and attune to these speed bumps increase your strengths. This adaptiveness, you must believe, will be an ally, not a weakness. Above all, it takes relentless positive energy, always attacking. If you are lacking in this type of energy, your early focus toward coaching should be assisting another.

To develop winners, you must first get them to believe in you and then your program. You do this first by your actions. Your positive beliefs and your Spartan work ethics must be visual and real. "To try once, to try twice, is not enough, suffice it to say, to sacrifice at any price will be enough." For the want of this is the main reason that so many coaches fail. One afternoon, while catching crawdads with Dr. Dale Thomas, Hall of Fame wrestling coach, he said, "You can't be a successful coach without thinking about coaching every day."

Your equal concerns over your players' wants and needs have to be sincere. Your goals and their early goals must be attainable. Pie-in-the-sky type of goals can be devastating to a team. Your goals at first must be simple and rewarding types of goals. Team goals need to be attained first. They can be sophisticated goals designed by a diverse team committee, or they can be simple, chartable types of goals composed by your players and agreed upon by the team. It is necessary that all personnel, players, managers, trainers, statisticians, all people connected with the team have a say in your goals. Keep these goals realistic and attainable. My 1996 team brainstormed, and then the team captains synthesized those ideas from the meeting. A lengthy and thoughtful pyramid using the team mascot materialized. (See page 155.)

Assemble some chartable goals. A few examples are, at every practice, continue shooting until your team eventually hits twenty lay-ins without a miss or, by the first game—as a team—be averaging a free-throw success rate of 70 percent or, by the fifth practice, have a goal that everyone can run ten ODs (an alternating offensive-defensive running drill) under sixty seconds. A more lofty goal might be, by winter break, your overall team grade point average shows a 10 percent increase. Practical goals such as by the first game, every different defensive trap can be demonstrated and executed by each player without any mistakes. Contest goals such as keeping uncontested turnovers under four in your first game and competing well in your first game. Common contest goals are winning the league. You win the last game your play: a very substantial goal, if you think about it. The goal to win lacks substance but it's better than a goal to play harder than the opponent, which is subjective and hard to measure.

Start recruiting in the fall for bench assistants, managers, game-book recorders, statisticians, video recorder, and trainer/taper. These assistants can make your coaching duties less complicated. Be careful of your selections; do not let them be influenced out of desperation. It is important to select them early and have that process completed before the season nears. Your choices can be a season-long blessing or a season-long curse, so be prudent in your decision-making process. A look at these candidates' academic standing would be a logical first step, for you are not choosing them for their athletic prowess. Make certain that they have good work habits and that their parents support this activity. Once selected, treat them no differently than your players. Involve them in all of your off-court team activities. Inform your players that they are to be treated with the same respect as any other member of the team. I am not posturing about this; this equal treatment falls under the "weakest link in the chain" simile. Camelot aspirations aside, it is just the right thing to do.

Your program needs to be structured and visible. It is difficult to display on paper, but what is shown must add up to the reader. Near the end of every practice, when your players are tired, present situations for them to solve. Oral pop quizzes during a dead-ball situation. For example, just about the time that a player is throwing in the ball on an out-of-bounds play is a timely and useful moment for some quizzing. Expect correct answers. These quizzes are beneficial for determining your team's mental focus and for keeping them mentally prepared. Questions like what's the score, who is in foul trouble, are we in the one-and-one bonus or two-shot bonus, are there any mismatches on the floor, do we have any fouls to waste, what defense has the opponent been using, are they switching defenses, what defense should we expect to see, do the opponents have a foul problem we should challenge, how many time-outs do we have? This may seem like overkill, but it can be done quickly and will be important to all concerned. Before our players were eligible to play in a game, no matter how many practices they had participated in, they had to pass a written test with a perfect score. If they failed, they could attempt it again the next day. Of course, our tests (see pages 157-158) were slanted toward our philosophies. The answers to the questions were repeatedly discussed in our first week's practice.

All of this demonstrates to your players the sincerity and seriousness of the program. It may seem here to the reader that we as coaches might be making the process a little too complicated. Relax—you might be right. I remember sitting with Ralph Miller and a few other coaches while absorbed over a glass of scotch whisky on the rocks, Ralph's favorite drink. I remember him sarcastically blurting out, "Listen here, all of you young—s. Quit trying to make the game so—damn difficult." He also went on to proclaim, "There has been nothing new, offensively and defensively, in basketball in forty years. Keep the game simple." This, by a hall-of-fame coach who personally met the creator of basketball, Dr. James Naismith.

Any team successes should be posted, announced, magnified, and celebrated between coaching staff and players. Everywhere your players go, they should be reminded of their success, however small it might be. A league championship banner should be hung in the gym, one at each end, one in the locker room, one in the school hallway, a copy of one on your team's practice jerseys (see below), a statement of such on your team's medical kit box, a statement of such on any fliers that originate from your office. *Do not be modest about team success!*

These constant mnemonics, reminders, are to develop an association with winning by your players. Their believing in themselves as winners is decisive.

Shell out a few bucks on Burger King value meals for those cardboard crowns, and let your players wear them at practice during lay-in drills. Your players will feed off these goodies and believe the attention, as they should and as you want.

It's exciting to take a new program and build. There are many steps in building a program. It's not just within the high school program. It involves working at many levels. It involves working with volunteers—training those volunteers and building trust between them and your program. You will have many who will volunteer to assist you, and many will expect coaching freedom—freedom to experiment and to guide in their own personal manner. This is where the trust comes in.

You must pay close attention to your program's outside interests. Be careful of support groups, booster committees, and rally groups. The more time, support, and funds they give, the more they feel control and the more obligated you feel. Collectively, they can make much happen for your team; but on downtimes, they can turn into an organized vigilante group. "Victories have a hundred fathers, defeat is an orphan." Your ideal support group would not be an orphanage.

Another outside interest you must culture and develop is the media. Be their friend. Their late evening sports deadlines are very serious. You can help them and be rewarded with positive coverage by making sure your late calls are accurate and concise. Double-check your figures, and present them orderly. There is nothing more upsetting to a sports reporter then having to take extra time from their busy schedule correcting your numbers. When addressing the media, especially when coaching girls, have two players phone in the evening game results and statistics. The players enjoy it, and the male reporters love it. Counsel and advise your phone people to make certain that others on the team will get their names in and that pertinent and relative facts get in. *I guarantee your team will get more ink!* Let all concerned know of this policy. This will quell any fan problems with coaches' favorites getting all the publicity.

Most schools require one or two parent-player-coaches meetings at the start of the season and before games begin. I might first suggest, especially to young coaches, to *stay away from making close friends with parents. You will thank me for this later.* As parents get closer to you, they seem to feel more obliged to share their basketball knowledge with you. Giving, especially on an early date, any partial promises to parents, ascertaining that their child will be getting quality time on the floor is foolhardy and professional suicide. Assure the parents, because of your extreme competitive nature, that the best players that can give you the ability to win will start regardless of their personal affiliations. Hold two meetings: the first to discuss the team-parent agreement with its rules and consequences, which should be given out early to the players for their parents to peruse and sign. (See pages 159-163.)

At both meetings, bring close attention to that portion of the team creed, "Remember, once you become a member of a team, you must forfeit many individual rights . . ." Butler University says it in similar fashion. The Butler Way: "The Butler Way demands commitment, denies selfishness, accepts reality, yet seeks improvement everyday while putting the team above self." This is a good time for asking their (parents) support to your creed and to your team calendar. Request them to coordinate their calendars with your team calendar for the upcoming season. This will squelch any undesirable future surprises.

Prepare a letter to the parents as a welcome to the program, as a preview of the first meeting, and enclose a copy of their player's agreement in case they missed it. (See page 164.)

At the first meeting, present the first month's practice schedule (see page 165) and the game schedule (see page 166). Our first months' practice schedule, which was in November, announced when the first presentation of certain skills and techniques would occur.

Again, use this first meeting to present a very brief philosophy statement toward the program and its design. Do not present your value determination with regard to evaluating your players. You could probably not concretely substantiate this decision-making process anyway. Mention that you will enjoy meeting again at the team's upcoming intersquad scrimmage. Do not volunteer a question-answer period; if they have any questions, you will hear them. Unrehearsed open dialogues should be avoided, so keep it short. A statement such as, "If there are any uncertainties regards the aforementioned topics, you are personally sure that they will be presented and covered in a practicum manner at your next meeting, which will be on the practice floor." This will wrap up and polish up the meeting nicely. Oh, lest I forget, remind them that changes to the calendars, which you just handed out, will occur often throughout the year but that you will do everything possible to contact them before such changes. A simple but popular item with players, parents, and fans are wallet calendars (see below). Little cost for the convenience and pleasure received (additional examples on page 167).

The above is a sample of our season schedule with a simple team picture on the opposite side. We had them made at a local office supply store. For a minimal cost, these items brought much enjoyment to the team and fans. They were handy and practical. The team looked forward each year to select the team picture site. We tried posing in front of a Boeing 747s on our flight to Hawaii but, alas, Homeland Security saw the action as a security breach of national consequences. We understood?

On our way to our first game of the 2000 season, while passing through Vernonia, Oregon, we spotted this old locomotive in their city park (above). We stopped the bus; someone on the bus had a digital camera, and the bus driver took our team picture. We took it to a local office supply company, we had our season schedule printed on the backside, and presto—behold.

If you have a team Web site, this would be a good time to peruse it with their parents. To solve many of the communication problems that accompany verbal sources, we elected to build a team Web site. This solved many problems that had plagued us over past years. The Web site included schedules, calendars, team member profiles, team history, team records, pictures, recent game synopsis, game predictions, ten most outstanding game memories, and more information than most people cared about. This action was good, for it covered everything imaginable and saved the coaching staff from many inquisitive calls. It was time consuming to begin with, but fortunately for us, it was mostly volunteer help that designed and maintained the site. Our school computer teacher assigned the composing of the site as a class project. They also continued to update it weekly. (See page 168 for an example of our 1997 Web site front page.)

Anyone that has worked with children can understand the communication problems related to messages conveyed by students to their parents. You might as well rely on the accuracy of a grapevine system at a school for the deaf. This Web site was an immediate, "Why did we wait so long?" I highly recommend, if you haven't already established a site, your perusal and pursuit of the same should be a program-building priority. Your school board officials will celebrate over it. My past problems with school boards, over all of my basketball programs, have been 99 percent related to communication errors between myself, my coaching staff, my players, and parents. This site has reduced and almost eliminated those problems.

Parents appreciate your thinking of them in your coaching and planning for the players. A good rapport between you and parents is paramount. A good example of how this can work for you and the team is practice on Thanksgiving Day, which is a taboo time to interfere between player and family. I also believe this. I also believe that if you are not practicing, someone else is. So at the first parent—coach's meeting, I always threw out the idea of helping mom on Thanksgiving Day. "Mom, how would you like your son out of the kitchen on Thanksgiving morning, out of your hair, and out from under your feet? I propose to have an 8:00 a.m. practice. We will end at ten. If he was at home, he would likely still be in bed at that time." Seldom have I heard a negative reply to this furtive suggestion. The opposite. Most mothers said, "Take him. That's a great idea. I love that idea." Soon, this anomaly became a team tradition. Other coaches, on hearing that we always practiced on Thanksgiving, could not believe it. It was all in the parent rapport, good communications, and trust that we had built. One time, for some reason, the players elected to practice on Friday rather than on Thanksgiving Thursday. I brought five or six garbage cans to intersperse around the floor. These were for buffering the excessively pumpkin-pie-filled tummies with our usual macabre running drills. The next year, we were back to Thanksgiving morning practice.

At your second parent meeting, which is during your intersquad practice, as the players are going through their warm-ups and drills, you should carry a microphone to emcee the action. You need to explain what the players are doing and why. A required nuisance that will be short-lived for that year. Thank the parents for their attendance, support; and solicit their positive reinforcement of the program with their child. Parental negative comments regarding coaching should be for the coach's ears only. Positive reinforcement at home is as important as positive statements at practice. Negative comments should be directed to the coaches. Parents need to be urged to support their coaches when speaking to their children. A negative dialogue between parent and player has no culmination compared to what positive results can come from a timely call between parent and coach. It is to be hoped that no reminders will be needed for the rest of the year.

During this practice session, make certain there are many different one-on-one match-ups; these will exploit vividly to your audience your personnel weaknesses. A great drill for this is, and I assume you have six baskets in your gym, start a game of one-on-one at each basket. After sixty-seconds, have the winners rotate clockwise to the next basket. Losers stay at home. Continue this for ten minutes. Some players will become mired down and never leave a basket. Others will circle the entire gym floor. Parents who watch their child stumble and fumble through this drill will better understand the evaluative judgment behind your early personnel decisions. This possibly will foster support and help at home for any deficiencies observed. Obviously, your personnel decision-making involves much more than one-on-one skills, but it is a useful starting tool for evaluating your talent. I have had many great one-on-one players who never started for me. This obligated second meeting with the parents has been conducted at no expense from your players workout time. Clever, huh?

Approximately a week before your first game, have a Civil War game (intersquad contest). Organize it so that each quarter, different players are alternated with different players. Invite the band and your cheerleaders. Open up concessions, and have official referees. These officials seldom charge your school and will look forward for their new referees getting some game experience before the real thing. Ask the referees if they might be willing to give a short clinic on the points of interests and new rules for the current year.

Charge a minimum fee as a team moneymaker for funding future trips. This game is very important for the players and for the coaches. There is nothing like the real thing, such as game fouls, to evaluate where your team's aggressiveness level is before its first contest. Little technical things become exploited, which would, in a real game, be costly. At halftime, retire to the locker room to discuss those items pertinent to the game—keep it to regulation time. Once the full regulation time has passed, regardless of the score, change the scoreboard back to zero and remove any time on the clock. There will be little expense to players' confidence if there is any lopsided scoring. Once the contest is over, ask the referees for a short extended period dictated by sudden-death rules. First team to score wins! This always leaves the game on a light note, and the players love it, and so do the fans.

Once the season begins, after each game, I always recognized the winner of the Eraser Award in the school's morning bulletin. The award went to the player who had the most steals in that game. (We also included blocked shots in the steals.) *We prohibited our players from blocking shots in the first quarter.* A high percentage of your blocked shots are seen as fouls by referees. Violators of our first-quarter-no-foul rule were immediately benched. Eliminating these imbecilic adrenaline-motivated infractions aided us in keeping our personnel into the latter, more important time periods. As the year went on, our players seemed to play more intelligently. Due to this restriction, in part, I believe that their overall court decisions improved in these early parts of the game. Too bad we weren't smart enough to implant something that caught their attention in the latter-time periods. At the end of the season, at our awards banquet, I awarded a new classroom eraser to our player who led the team in steals and blocked shots.

The Golden Shoe Award was also announced in the morning bulletin. It went to the player with the most turnovers in the game. The general student body did not know, I don't think, what the award symbolized. I took a very old and battered discarded Nike basketball shoe and spray painted it gold. It looked really repulsive. The day after the game, the winner picked it up from my office and carried it to classes until lunch hour. It was like I was with the carrier all morning, continually reminding that player to be more careful when in control of the ball. It was all done in good humor and not done to disgrace or embarrass the carrier. No recipient had to wear it at practice or out on dates. I saw to it no one carried it three times in a row. I also let parents know of this practice at our first parent-player-coach meeting. No big deal—just some fun at the expense of butterfingers!

To your players, be brutal; advise them that you will rank them throughout the year as to their value to the team by the order their name is placed in the green game book. Inform them that this will not be in ink, but written in pencil, which is easily erasable, and that you sincerely hope that many erasures occur. The more smudgy our green book becomes, the stronger our team becomes. Every time we erase and reenter, our team becomes more balanced from bottom to top. You should give no false illusions to your players; after the initial bluntness of their team standing with you, they will learn to appreciate your openness, and they will not be kept dangling throughout the year and throughout each game wondering if they will get in. Your early abruptness is more humane than any other alternative pretense. Again, be brutally frank. On the home front, for your spouse's benefit, ease up on the frankness: buy a dog to kick around during the season.

When you have had a good hard practice, reward by reducing conditioning. After a lax practice, follow up with defensive-offensive shuffles until the cows come home. When do cows come home, where do they go? Your running and conditioning drills should be applicable to the needs of the game. If you plan on a fast-breaking style of game plus a pressing type of defense, you obviously are going to need much aerobic conditioning. Our sprinting drill involved running to the far end of the court and returning, doing a defensive shuffle. Sixteen distances within sixty seconds. If someone could not make it, then we would take a fifteen-second rest, and then do it again. Interspersed between sprints, while resting, we executed a few various plyometrics. Normally, by the fifth practice, every player becomes successful. I personally believe our early OD running drills were harder mentally than physically. Once a player survives these early drills, they come to rationalize that there is life after the drill, then they start believing they can do more and do them faster. We know, as coaches, if we design our practices to be less exhausting than our games, we are preparing our players for failure. It is music to our ears when we hear from our players that the games are easy compared to our practices. It is our confirmation as coaches that our practices are more than adequately focused toward the contests.

On a normal practice session, from our circle drill through dribbling, then through our full-court lay-in drill, all interspersed with ODs, our players run for twenty minutes. This is where every member on the team earns a vested interest in the team's success. They personally convert their ideology to a common tenet to have not worked this extremely hard to lose!

When coaching girls, be careful what you instruct them. At this time, they are more tunneled in their vision than boys. Schools have not had girls' basketball programs for as long as the boys. You better know your stuff, for they are going to do exactly what you say or what you present to them. At this current period in basketball, girls are less likely to wing it than boys. So again, be careful what you tell them because that is likely what they are going to do. Also, be careful how you tell them—their emotions are carried right out there on their sleeves.

Ralph Miller, hall of fame college basketball coach, stated to me in the confines of his office, "Bill, if I had it all to do again, I would go into coaching college girls' basketball to skip all the bullshit that goes with coaching boys." I respected the wisdom of Coach Miller, but I also realized the man had never coached girls.

Be imaginative. It is easy to follow the path of others, and one should do so after sorting and sifting their ideas. What normally works best is what works well for you. By that, I mean that some things that work well for your mentors or other coaches may not work for you for many reasons. Don't hesitate using your own ideas, especially those imagined while watching your own practice and watching your own talent. "Greater than the tread of mighty armies is an idea whose time has come"—Victor Hugo. Your intuition and/or wildest ideas should be entertained, at least once, but not necessarily twice.

To build team unity, my coaching staff developed many outside activities to involve our players, events outside the realm of hoops. Woman Haters Week was one example. To keep a team focused on a particular game, the coaches would choose a particular game and assign that week as Woman Haters Week. No one was allowed to change outer clothes during this week and was not allowed to talk to a girl outside of the classroom. The premise was to keep your No break from it, not even to select clothes for the day. Anyone caught changing clothes or talking to a girl by another varsity member automatically received an OD (an offensive-defensive drill that players quite OD'd from). All violators would have to run their OD's at the last practice of Woman Haters Week.

Another activity was KK's (Kris Kringle's). The week before Christmas break, all team members drew a name from a hat. The name drawn was kept very quiet. For the player drawn, they had to buy a cheap gift each day of the week and somehow pass it secretly to that person. They could not be observed passing the gift by another varsity member; an OD penalty was assigned if they were caught. On the last day of that week, at our team Christmas party, everyone had to guess who their secret Santa was; and if they were incorrect, they were assigned an OD. If they were correct with their guess, their KK donor was assigned two OD's. The players had fun with this charade. They would try to trick each other. An example of a ruse was one player giving their daily gift to an unconcerned player and asking that player to be observed passing it on to the rightful donee. The idea of this deceit was, of course, to confuse and create a wrong guess. After all the deceit, you probably intuitively sense some counterproductive efforts to our goal of unifying the team. During this period, I never saw our team members so close, and it was considerable fun.

The mornings of a home game, we celebrated together by eating as a team at a local restaurant. The rooks or any new members to the varsity provided entertainment. Individually, they had to recite a poem of their own making or sing a song of their own making. The verses had to be about the team we were playing that evening. While they were reciting or singing, they had to stand with their left leg off the ground while holding their left earlobe in their right hand. After each performance the whole team thumbed up or down regards their performance. A Roman gladiator evaluative carryover, a majority of thumbs down meant the reciter or singer would have to compose a new program for our next breakfast. A majority of thumbs up meant the artist was excused for the remainder of the season. This seldom happened. The extremely bad or boring were sometimes excused to relieve our own anguish. Quite often, the exceptionally good ones were thumbed down so we could further feast on their talent. By word of mouth and by popular demand, some players ended up entertaining at our school pep rallies. Some players ended up entertaining right through the state championships.

Once a season, in appreciation of their support, we invited the cheerleaders to our breakfast on the condition that they came prepared to entertain us. They always seemed flattered and ate and entertained robustly. Our players always seemed to have mixed emotions about their visit.

We also had a bring-a-favorite-teacher breakfast. This was a favorite. The smart player worrying about academic eligibility could tactfully use this for their own personal gain. They certainly had nothing to lose by it.

One senior, at a time, hosted a team dinner or barbecue at their home. If you have only one senior on your team, this will obviously have little effect. We worked hard at making appreciation gestures to the cheerleaders and song leaders. Following each game, after immediately shaking hands with the opponents, we instructed our players to cross over the gym to acknowledge our pompom-toting faithful by also shaking their hands.

My recommendations regards filming your games for future contests is to film only the second half. This half will include the adjustments made after halftime, which is probably what will incur the next time you play this team. This will save you much editing time. For your players, cut and paste highlights from the game such as problems, errors, and positive pieces. Do not share the whole game with the team; rather, you should repeatedly use this edited shorter cut. Your players will appreciate these periods more and will be more serious about them. Preparing this method will take some editing time, but it will be well worth it. As a coach, you will accomplish more coaching over the game with this edited version in much less time, which will allow you to get back on the floor quicker.

A few last statements on building a basketball program: Do not share your gym time with others. If the athletic director mentions or suggests that your team shorten their practices, you better get to the negotiating table immediately. If it ends up that your team is faced with less practice time than your opponents, you are going to lose games to them. If necessary, have practices at 5:00 a.m. Basketball is a game that becomes accomplished through practices. A quick analogy: Take your local Sasquatch down from the hill, and strap a helmet to his head. And you have, with the proper motivation, an instant all-league tackle. Put the same hairy all-league tackle on the basketball court, and watch the debacle. Five years later, watch the fun. You must practice. It is imperative that you become hard-nosed and stingy to all when it comes to your practice time. Be proactive from the start. When you are hired, suggest they refinish the gym floor over spring break instead of summer, if they don't already. If they don't, ask why. This is not negotiable. Summer basketball, unfortunately, has become a necessary part of building a competitive basketball program. You become almost obligated to extend basketball over this period because others schools do.

Rather than leave our chargers to the summer pandering philosophical pedagogues of dubious basketball lessons, we opted to teach our players personally. We knew one thing for sure: what we knew and what they should know for best preparing themselves for our program. A second thing we knew: if they were going to pay for a summer basketball camp, why shouldn't we be the donees? We named our endeavor the Snappin' Twine Camp. We used most of the fees received for subsidizing our school varsity team trips. The swishing sound of the basketball going through the net to the average wannabe NBA-er is like Mozart to the music buff. So rather than doing disservice to the hearing gifted and describing its sound, we deferred to describing it visually. (See pages

169-170 for our flyer.) We distributed these in our school and at other local schools, YMCA, and public recreational outlets. We also advertised in the local revolutionary rags (newspapers).

After some years of providing as much summer basketball entertainment in a week that we could conjure up, we recognized that we were just prostituting ourselves. We decided to change our camp structure from drawing as large a population as possible to marketing just our own school's students and formatting the camp to mirror our varsity practices. We selected four skills that we felt were most important and that would mesh for our program and for their improvement. These skills we taught repeatedly. To keep the campers challenged and not bored, we took these skills and encompassed them into the other skill drills. We presented some of the varsity's plays. We ran the camp drills and games competitively yet still monitoring that our newly taught skills were being used. We endeavored to send the campers home wet and tired.

Our Snappin' Twine Camp became very successful. We could see the benefits of it early in our winter practices. As a team, it put us a week ahead in our practice schedules. Even though many players could not attend the Snappin' Twine, their individual progress seemed to be accelerated by those who did attend.

Rather than comatose on football during the fall, which is fun, we as coaches decided to continue dabbling in basketball for the profit of our players. In our state, it is illegal to meet with more than two basketball players per day for basketball instruction. If you were to coordinate this time between all of those who aspire to play varsity, excluding football players, and to those who salivate at the sound of a bouncing basketball, you would end up meeting the same players over the fall about four times. Not much can be accomplished in this limited time. We decided to put our time and efforts into a Ways and Means project to improve our basketball schedule and to use these monies for our varsity trips.

Each year, my coaching staff would attend a statewide coaching clinic. These were normally sponsored by basketball corporate endorsers such as Gatorade or Nike. Ex-pros or college coaches were normally the guest speakers. Guest speakers, remember that term. We noticed that during the overhead diagrams of X's and O's, many in the audience—college coaches, high school coaches, junior high coaches, grade school coaches, and basketball fans—were either lost, bored, or just asleep. Watching coaches inscribe little out-of-focus X's and O's on overheads with a running dialogue compares to studying slow-motion techniques of vertical jumping by the North American slug.

The thought of a clinic focused for only high school coaches seemed like a desirable and practical venture. A profitable venture for both the coaches and the organizers. Well, how hard could that be? This seemed to be a natural endeavor for our empty fall months. The Snappin' Twine Clinic was born. In our state, a teachers in-service date falls in October. This was a perfect time for running a basketball clinic, which was coincidentally only a few weeks before the state approved opening date of practices.

We started off small with local high school coaches as guest speakers. Later years, we dropped the overheads and used players to run the guest coaches' drills and plays. Later, when the rule of only two players a day could assemble with a high school coach, we were stretched for imaginative concurrences. As pawns for the guest lecturers, we brought in two players from five different schools, which kept us within our state's governing edicts. If you consider running a project such as this, make certain you go with the players rather than the overheads. This visual type of presentation was easy to understand and interesting to follow. Our clinic became popular due to this live format change. Our costs were limited to sandwiches and drinks, which our cheerleaders organized and reaped the profits from. The school gym was free of cost. Our varsity players provided the setting up and various physical tasks such as enrolling, guides, and cleaning up—for which they were rewarded. They indirectly profited from the lectures and presentations that they were able to listen to and watch. Local sports ventures readily provided us with items for raffles. To our surprise, sportswear and sports equipment companies paid us to set up displays at our clinic. Each year, we included a coaches' crude job placement center (table). Coaching positions throughout the state were listed. This was a popular station.

Earlier, I referred to guest speakers; by our third or fourth year, we began soliciting college coaches. These guest speakers surprised us by treating us as guests, asking for no payment. So from then on, the speaker format changed to college coaches or ex-pros speaking to our high school coaching audience, with high school players demonstrating the X's and O's. (See page 171 for a copy of our year 2000 clinic.)

Our last two years of sponsoring the Snappin' Twine Clinic brought in approximately two hundred coaches. Our local community college gave a physical education credit for completion of the six hours. Because of the few expenses, we were able to keep the enrollment costs to a fraction of that charged by the clinics of corporate organizers. Try this moneymaking venture for your team. It is not that difficult, especially for the rewards received.

Scheduling summer basketball games can be a nightmare. Waiting until spring to phone coaches is a mistake. Most coaches are teachers and cannot be reached during the day; phone tag always ends up with nobody knowing who is it. My Advil suggestion is to draft a summer schedule in the fall. Include a signup sheet for soliciting teams during the winter when you are personally reaching coaches at your games. Draft a return postcard for handing out to the noncommittal, wishy-washy type of coaches. Your dates should be for home tournaments. Coaches are more inclined to spend their summer weekends at your gym when they are guaranteed three or four games. Another suggestion: make these tournaments no cost for the visitors. You can do this by requesting the visiting coaches or their assistants to officiate the game before theirs. This no-fee idea works well because normally, enrolling in a summer tournament is very expensive. After our no-fee tournaments and after coaches recognized they could survive the rigors of half-court refereeing, we routinely heard the following requests, "Please invite us back next year."

An advantage of holding your own summer program is that you are keeping your students from attending an expensive independent summer basketball camp. My experience at independent summer basketball camps, clinics, and academies is that most of these cater to the wishes of the players. No new skill drills; nothing but scrimmaging and games are played. Most of these camps are glorified overnight high-priced baby-sitting bivouacs. Most players are not there of their own accord. Their parents have deposited them for a period of well-earned comforting solace. I have often thought of how much money could be made by a reformatted basketball camp that truly appealed to the youngsters. This camp would present no perspiring activities, no sudden ballistic-type drill or exercise movements, no man-to-man defensive principles, zone defenses only, sprinkled with "bump" games and highlight videos. A fortune could be made at these camps. Registration lines would rival Splash Mountain's.

In finishing this chapter on building a successful basketball program, I recommend you focus your thoughts as a true capitalist. As any business establishment knows, an annual efficiency determination is justified. It is no different with a basketball program. A win-loss record is an extrinsic measurement. Many factors need to be analyzed. How are you measuring your program's success? Achieving your team goals can be misleading. Your program might be successful in spite of your undertakings; possibly an unusual class of excellent athletes are currently present. Your success might be short-lived without a closer analysis of the structure and its results. A close look of your organization needs unattached outside opinions; it needs an honest personal assessment from all coaches. It will profit from periodic self-evaluating devices, tools that monitor whether short-term objectives are being met, tools that measure personal athletic progress and the players' personal needs.

One tool that has provided us much useful information was a follow-up questionnaire for the players to answer. We tried to format the form not to be too invasive or too personal, lest inhibiting or creating hesitance of what we hoped to be factual and useful responses. (See example page 172-173.)

Another tool and probably our most reliable indicator of success was our turnout numbers and dropout rate. If your program has maximum interest and maintains its participants, you are heading in the right direction, regardless of the wins and losses. Continue what you are doing—the wins are going to come. If you are new to coaching, be prepared for the questions of less ardent followers. You might find your program excelling in most areas; but I guarantee you, no matter how much you feel your program is meeting the motivational needs of your players, you must expect the following: "Coach, are we running much tonight?" I guarantee you by the third or fourth query of this nature, you will not want to tackle untangling bungee cords while wearing mittens. Nothing will test your mental framework or challenge your serenity posture more than the constant query of "Coach, are we running much tonight?" I heard this so much, I always wanted to respond, "Why are you here?" Fearful of hearing a philosophical retort such as "Because of the Big Bang," I would turn to avoid such responses.

Once, after conducting a brief meeting on proper greetings, I started hearing such questions as, "Hello, Coach. How are you? How is your family?" and before I could answer, "Coach are we running much tonight?" Well, it was an improvement.

Chapter 2

Travel

For creating unity, every year, we planned a Christmas holiday basketball trip. Depending on the calendar, we would travel between December 26 and January 2. By waiting to depart on the twenty-sixth or twenty-seventh, we avoided any controversy of leaving families over Christmas. We looked for tournaments with two or three games. There is no trouble finding these contests; they abound. Tactful letters sent to parents at least six months ahead allows for their planning and eliminates surprises. Parents hate surprises; however, surprises are tempered when they are not accompanied by money requests. Our trips were extremely economical because we largely subsidized our meals on my wife's homemade turkey jerky and we toted sleeping bags for sleeping in gyms, school stages, Home Ec rooms, and wrestling rooms. To find the best competition, we have traveled many times from Oregon to Los Angeles or to Seattle, four times to Hawaii, once to Denver, and twice to Las Vegas (a Mecca for holiday basketball tournaments). Generally, it only took the preceding summer and fall to fund these excursions.

Some of our best moneymakers were (1) at local timber-clearing cuts, planting Douglas fir seedlings and after thinning operations on timber lands, selling Christmas trees; (2) at the local shopping mall where we set up a gift-wrapping operation; (3) at the local I-5 interstate rest stop area, providing coffee for donations. A good long holiday weekend could net you a thousand dollars. A great place for meeting some real colorful characters. Rest stops have a culture of their own. This endeavor was by far our most lucrative, at no cost and little effort. A future moneymaker would be working both sides of the interstate and dropping our other less profitable efforts. I guess putting all our eggs in one basket would alleviate any burnout from too many endeavors.

There was little problem about amassing enough funds—the difficult part was finding chaperones for these activities. Another stumbling block was smoothing the conservative naysayers who probably never dared a venture more daring than a backyard tent lifting. The common negative excuse for a trip was the old echo of school liability. The first time we invited a school board member to accompany us on one of our trips, he, fortunately for us, made it back alive; and we never had a future trip request denied. A warning: no matter how far in advance you notify parents, many will decide at the last minute to accompany your team on your trip to see the games. They assume you have a travel bureau's license and that you will be prepared to facilitate their whims. You will need to be prepared to tactfully explain why you didn't reserve extra emergency flight tickets. They cost money and are not refundable!

What does this have to do with building a program? The word of traveling spreads. Our middle school players were excited for their next level of play, in part, due to the stories they heard about the high school trips. Each year, the competition was a frenzy for a traveling varsity position. The word of our habit of going on exciting trips increased our player turnouts.

We always went by public transportation, airlines, or Amtrak. Public transportation was a stress reliever for our school board. Our means of travel was insured and the school's yellow buses were not put at risk plus the out-of-state liability posed by these trips was eliminated.

The residual benefit of these hoop treks was camping in a gym. You woke in the gym, you napped in the gym, and you fell asleep in the gym. Between these nightcaps, there is not much to do but shoot baskets in the gym. There are few televisions, if any. Your practices are uninterrupted and can go on forever. No one has to go home early or even go home for that fact. "As a coach, ya gotta love it!" You have your players away from home and all their electronic devices. No traveling surprises by mom and dad are going to interrupt practices. Your players' favorite aunts and uncles are not dropping in. Little petty reasons for missing practice are eliminated. You have them under your basketball umbrella for a whole week of unadulterated coaching. These are great periods and situations for presenting and practicing new ideas. Much can be accomplished during this time.

For a little cultural diversity on these trips, we always ordered Chinese food in and rented the video *Mr. Bean Goes on Vacation,* an economical and simple gesture appreciated by parents and school board members. The fun and memories from a trip like this are usually echoed for all to hear in our school hallways. The events are noteworthy enough to usually find a page or two in the school annual.

These winter contests abound, but finding the best talent to play is somewhat difficult. Finding these games is especially difficult for small schools. Larger schools do not want play down in size. Successful teams from small schools do not want to risk their records against a larger team. The "dammed if you win, and damned if you lose" parody for large schools comes into play. Large schools, on the other hand, must look hard and far for competitive games. If you are allowed to travel far distances, it becomes much easier to pick more desirable games. Preseason games are extremely important games for challenging your team. It is important for your team's growth to schedule equal or better talent. This is a period where you want your weaknesses exploited so you can ascertain your progress and correct any deficiencies before you start your league games.

There are limitations to playing up. I took a team to Fullerton, California, in the late '80s for a holiday tournament. We were from Oregon, and we traveled by Amtrak. The trip involved much organizing and early scheduling. Upon our arrival, we were notified that our first contest of the tourney was cancelled an hour earlier by our opponents. The tourney coach was very helpful in assisting us find a replacement team to play. He contacted a coach from either Mater Dei or Verbin Dei, I don't remember which. I am sure you have heard of both teams. I believe it was a boarding school, which, by its manner, presents high quality students, especially athletes.

Both of these schools are not unlike DeMatha High School of coach John Wooten fame. They do not lose many games. On talking with the coach of this potential opponent, he asked what size we were. I didn't care what the size of his school was—I always believed in playing up. I told him our school size. He confided with me that they had a six-foot-ten center who played for their junior varsity. He could not make the varsity. This was not to the center's lack of ability but because of the amazing talent on their varsity. We opted to pass on the varsity; we played the junior varsity team. I am a realist.

Against my better feelings, we traveled to Hawaii in 1984 to participate in three games unassociated with each other. We had expected to play in a high school tournament on the campus of Chaminade University, but these games were cancelled for reasons beyond my memory. Thus we ended up traveling across the Pacific Ocean to play schools our own size composed of mediocre to average talent. Granted, the trip was beautiful for many reasons. It just was not what we were looking for philosophically and physically. Boy, was I wrong. The lessons learned by our players in handling and abiding by the raving, biased lunacies of the island referees was worth college credit. Nowhere could you find a better analogy for the definition of *handicap*. Not a waste was this trip. Conditioning wise, it was also truly a timely experience. Never had we played in such heat. Our practice court times were at high noon. Our games were scheduled for high noon. Our players supplemented their thirst between, before, and after meals with shaved ice, an island favorite. (See photo.) Two days earlier, we had just slid over two hundred cold miles on snow-covered roads to the airport. Unbelievable.

In 1992, I took a girls' team to Hawaii. If you know anything about high school basketball in Hawaii, you know that they split their seasons for boys' basketball and girls' basketball. I did not know that. In a year advance when our athletic director scheduled our games with the Hawaiian athletic director, because of the timing over holiday break, they scheduled us in the boys' tournament,

assuming we were talking about boys, again because of the date. Their athletic director blocked out the sound "girls." The fiasco was only beginning. We stayed at Punahoe High School. On talking with the principle from Punahoe High School, our athletic director described our players as a great, almost-angelic group but, alas, a poor lot. Somehow, the name of our school went f rom Alsea High School to Saint Alsea School, I assume, an acceptable nomenclature for making school approval of our stay over easier. What to our surprise when told that the girls do not begin practicing until February, this being December. What a surprise to their athletic director when he saw our girls unloading from vans. They were a type of Christian school, probably Catholic. It seems like most athletic Christian schools are Catholic or at least the successful ones. I was in shock at the time, so I never explored their doctrine. It didn't matter. Fortunately for us, it was not an all-boys school. They were very gracious and very helpful. After not being able to enlist even a girls' town team to play, we just played the boys. Ho-hum. Good experience for St. Alsea. We would have competed better if the handicap of new uniforms (see right photo) wasn't made necessary by the locals.

A humorous side note of this trip: In anticipation of the costs for food on this trip, I solicited Burger King for help. Our local Whopper franchise graciously accommodated us. Partly out of their generosity and for some free publicity from our trip, they gave us a Happy Meal box stuffed with burger certificates. I phoned different restaurants on the island of Oahu for assistance. A restaurant at Turtle Bay Resort graciously responded that they would indeed help us by providing beaucoup food. How exciting, a five-star-restaurant dinner. On a previous trip, I had seen their establishment and was quite impressed. It was beautiful, with hanging bamboo bridges, a false realistic looking volcano that spewed red lava under its bridges. The descriptions that I gave the girls of this place motivated their dressing to the hilt for dinner. We looked like a very large prom conglomerate, only without boys or a limousine. All our traveling on the island was on the transit bus system. It took us two hours one way to circumvent the island to get to this restaurant. I could hear the girl's oohs and aahs of appreciation as they spied the oncoming facility. As we walked in, tired and in our very now wrinkled best wear, the maitre d' greeted us with "We have been expecting you. You're late." After our long bus ride, this was the music we needed to hear. I was relieved to hear this greeting, terse as it might have been, fearing that anything else unexpected after this long marathon milk run would spoil the evening's festivities. We were there and starving. As numbed as I was from the ever-stopping, block-by-block diesel-smelling trip we had just endured, I could still identify the smell of prime rib and melted butter for the lobsters. "Oh, boy! Put on the bibs, light the candles, and enjoy!" "Barkeep, wine and food for my merry men!"

We followed the maitre d' through the restaurant. I was with a beautiful assemblage of finely dressed tall young women in high heels that caught the eye of many diners. Our path was confusing; the maitre d' led us through the eating area to an elevator in the hallway behind the main restaurant dining area. I assumed we were going to a private room readied for us. The elevator doors opened to disclose a service lift with crates of produce. We entered and rapidly descended to the basement kitchen where some of the employees were eating and working. Surely, this was a mistake. We were told the selection of the employee buffet was scarce due to the late hour. Rational thoughts were quickly processing in my mind: *Why should we receive anything more? Had I been delusional? Could I miraculously salvage this night?* I was so embarrassed for our young women, all dressed up, sequestered to this stainless steel kitchen with steam floating above their heads. I was becoming a little disconcerted over the hushed but barbed comments between my players with each other.

My hungry team, in disbelief, looked over the selection of a large three-beaned salad, a casserole of macaroni and cheese, hard rolls, and eight or nine well-done hamburger patties. Soon, those burger patties disappeared to the utter frustration of our hungriest—not as well-received, as I might add, as the Whoppers we had been eating all week. I could not blame my players for losing their savoir faire in this unique social affair. I felt the full blame. I truly felt like a martyr being sacrificed to placate the team's embarrassment. Further embarrassment compounded as the girls in their formal wear struggled to slide into those park like aluminum benches that were under and attached to the tables. I wondered if this evening would ever end. More than once, a voice was overheard from the working staff regard our overdressed ladies, "They must be part of the entertainment upstairs."

Back up in the parking lot, we were told that the bus back to Punahoe High School had just left. *Of course!* Because of the late hour, the bus system went to their night schedule. This meant it would be an hour before the next bus. Talk about the stink eye I got while waiting for our bus; their umbrage was completely understandable, for we still had a two-or-more-hour return trip to our sleeping bags at Punahoe High School. If it wasn't for the entertainment of the actions of two transvestites that got onto our bus, those stink-eye stares would have become tattooed to my neck.

I can't emphasize enough the benefits that our program experienced from our willingness, as a coaching staff, to take those extra efforts to provide our players with rewarding travel packages. I must say that the trips also generated additional interest to us, the coaches. I know that they contributed to our overall cohesiveness as a team and to our later game successes.

Chapter 3

Practice Tips and Hints

In random order, I will discuss a hodgepodge of general practice thoughts. Hold early season team meetings at your school lunch hour or just before practice time. Do not jeopardize precious practice time with your team with court assemblies, when with a little imagination, they could have been held at a different time and place than the gym. Practice time is pure business time, which in basketball is on the court rockin' and rollin'. Most seasons, you should expect losses of gym time; in fact, they occur annoyingly frequently. So to avoid compounding these situations, be proactive with team meetings.

Always exhaust your players; run your practices at a game tempo. Send your players home to their moms hot and wet. Your practices should simulate game situations right down to team discussions being handled like game time-outs. Practice begins for the coach yesterday. Immediately after each practice, some short notes should be taken regards what wasn't finished in practice, what needs arose, and suggestions for the next practice. When composing your practice schedules, *never understress the importance of repetition.* The importance of competition in drills and practice are paramount, but do not stress them at the expense of repetition. Include conditioning in all your drills. Make everything you do game related. No one standing still! Make a month's calendar of presentations of all plays for the first time and their respective dates. Use this calendar to verify your coverage of every situation possible that your team will see over the year (see page 17.) For personal skill improvement, reenter those first presentations in your practices for every future practice day. If the drill you are presenting is not one worth showing every day for the remainder of the season, you probably shouldn't be showing it. Monitor your players' needs and work those needs into all of your drills and warm-up exercises. Run practices like a game: have a running clock and scoreboard, complete with horn.

Instructions during practice should come in short periods much like game time-outs. Your court lectures should be laconic and ran on the floor; they should be timed to simulate the time-out periods you use in games. Get the players used to your quick approach, rapid explanations, and emotional demands; and they will be less likely to misunderstand something said in the confusion and noise of the real game. Not a time for subliminal-style messages. Players need this pressure during practice to become better listeners and to learn to pick up on your body language and nonverbal messages.

Now a hodgepodge of thoughts in a somewhat coherent presentation:

I kept my practice schedule on a 5 × 9 inch laminated form that I hung from my sweat suit in a quick-draw location. It was a form that included a checklist of my routines, first presentations, drills, game situations, starting and ending times, notes, and a court diagram on the back. (See illustration #1.) A copy of this should be hung in the locker room or team room before practice.

PRACTICE PLAN

Practice #_____ **Date_________**
Next Opponent________________________ **In ________ Days**
Time __________ Absent __________ __________ __________

Ball Handling Drills:
- -Circle(famous 8)
- -Clap catch
- -Shortpass(inches)

Shooting Drills:
- -1 arm layine
- -2 ball layin
- -OSU split the post
- -Pop step
- -"Ball-Ball-Ball"
- -Shoot-follow-"0"
- -Alley Oop
- -Full court layins
- -3 lane rush
- -free throw dribble
- -__________

Dribbling Drills:
- -2 by 2 by 2 by 2
- -Slide & Glide
- -Between legs
- -Behind back
- -Combination
- -Reverse pivot
- -Stutter step
- -Keep ball behind
- -backwardsdribble
- -full court 4 dribbles
- -__________

Defensive Footwork:
- -chaircarry
- -quick step
- -shuffle
- -gauntlet switching
- -elbow and foot step-over
- -ODS & Corners

Time	Drill	Notes
	1.	
	2.	
	3.	
	4.	
	5.	
	6.	
	7.	
	8.	
	9.	
	10.	
	11.	
	12.	
	13.	
	14.	
	15.	

Evaluations/Comments:

____

____

____

Suggestions fornext practice:

____

____

____

Def. Team Drills:
- - 3 x 4 Shell
- - cherry pick
- - NBA

Off. Team Drills:
- -Early Offence
- -Blitz (UCLA)
- -Duke
- -North Carolina

Offensive Plays:
M/M:
-Down,"3","2","44",Pig
Zone:
Hi-Lo, Box, High Post, "Herc"

Slow-Down:
- -Grapevine
- -Spread Down
- -Spread OSU
- -Spread"Herc"

In-Bounds Plays:
M/M:
- -Spider (score & enter)
- -Easy In
- -Tip Back & (Side Tandem)
- - (1-4) Against pressure

Zone:
- -Cube
- -Movingcircle
- -Pic under

Finishers:
- -Chase loose balls (full-ct)
- -Shoot to leave

Home Of The Wolverines

I'm not a big stretching advocate. Those coaches and conditioning experts who might be appalled and shocked by this statement, relax. Not a big deal. My teams still stretch but not as a required regimented discipline. When we do stretch, we do so ballistically, contrary to current popular methods. We do herky-jerky stretching movements to train the muscles for the athletic needs that they will later confront. I will later expound on our quasi-stretching session. Over my thirty-plus years of coaching, my teams have had, knock on wood, extraordinarily good luck avoiding serious athletic injuries. I am not a medical specialist by any means, but it just makes common sense to me that on preparing for contact sports, being too limber attracts the more serious injuries. While you are scoffing, and you are probably right doing so, I will attempt to explain. Let's look at the knee. If the tendons behind the joint are stretched to become very limber, then a sharp contact from the front is probably going to cause hyperextension. Consequently, I believe the excessive extension of the joint traumatizes the stabilizing ligaments more severely. In a contact sport, I felt—to eliminate any chance of potential cartilage damage—it was important to maintain some tautness in the tendons. A less flexible joint would probably eliminate the overextension and result in tearing a tendon before causing serious ligament or cartilage damage. Who knows? I just share with you my coaching experience and fortunate noninjury results.

Do you remember when doctors advised us on not swimming after eating? Do you remember the important seven food groups we were taught to consume daily? It is important. It is imperative to listen to medically trained professionals, but we also need to keep an open mind. I live in a forested region and often come upon resting deer. On spooking them from sleep, I have never seen one make its ballistically quick escape and come up lame from a quick-movement-induced injury. I don't mean to sound obvious and trite, and I'm probably as wrong as those conditioners in the '60s that claimed that weightlifting for basketball players would be counterproductive, creating muscle-bound players.

I just wish to share with the reader my own personal experiences. In our circle drill (see following news clipping photo #2), we progressed from warming up the small muscles first, and then we worked up to the bulkier muscles. I believe, if you are going to follow a stretching regimen, keep your special stretching needs and convalescing needs, such as taping, scheduled independently and finished by your formal practice time.

The following is a sample of our daily practice schedule and a breakdown of each drill involved. We started practice at half court with each player with a ball. Anyone late or out of proper practice attire for practice caused disciplinary action for the entire team, except for the perpetrator who sat and watched the discipline played out. It only took this action once or twice during the season to eliminate players being late or dressed improperly. Positioned around the center circle, my players went through their quasi-stretching drills while keeping their basketballs active. (The transition between the following suggested stretching activities should be short. Encompass your needs into these activities; use your imagination.)

deep in talent, brace for super year

(2)

This is a good time for coach-player nonsensical exchanges. All of our pre-scrimmage drills were designed to complement our offensive and defensive styles. They changed yearly to adopt to necessary changing philosophies, needs, talent, and to the coaches getting smarter. Coaches smarter—good example of an oxymoron?

1. Stretching high on their toes, with the ball over their heads, they slapped the ball between their hands as quickly and hard as possible, not allowing the ball to drop while maintaining their balance (30 seconds)
2. Bring the ball down to the neck area and circumvent the head as fast as possible while bending back and forth and sideways at the waist. (15 seconds)
3. Bring the ball down to the waist and quickly circumvent the body while actively reversing directions. (15 seconds)
4. Bent over, with legs spread far, figure eight the ball in and around the legs quickly as possible. Expand on that by releasing the ball and catching it in the figure eight motion before it touches the floor; again, expand on that with a front and back catch, keeping the ball alive and off the floor. (30 seconds)
5. In the same squatting position, dribble the ball in and around the legs. Expand to dribbling the ball very low between the knees and maintaining the ball's position directly under the torso. Alternate the hands from behind and in front of the knees while controlling the dribble of the ball. I attribute this drill to many recoveries of loose bouncing balls in congested areas. (30 seconds)
6. Now bend forward from the waist with legs spread sideways, and dribble back and forth one handed from foot to foot while alternating control of the ball with the back side and the front side of the hand. Each dribble should be a little longer in length. (30 seconds)
7. Next we would do front-to-back splits and dribble front to back. (30 seconds)
8. Drop to one knee with the other knee up with that thigh parallel to the floor. Continue a nonstop dribbling regimen under and over thigh and around the back. (1 minute)
9. Sit with legs spread, head between knees, and then maintain a finger dribble while alternating digits with emphasis on pushing and not slapping the ball. (30 seconds)
10. Lay on back while continuing the dribble. Bring the dribble up alongside the body and then around the head to the opposite waiting hand. Difficult drill. (30 seconds)

The above ball handling activities are to develop hand-eye coordination and to create established neural pathways, but most of all, ball handling confidence. I would suggest that a new exercise be introduced every other week to constantly keep your ball handlers challenged. Before our dribbling activities, all of our players engaged in the following coordination drill. Each player holds a small ball such as a tennis ball, softball, or golf ball. They would then take the ball in their right hand and lift their right leg. They would then take the ball under that leg and toss it up close and in front of their body to about eye level. While the ball was in the air, they dropped their right leg and lifted their left leg up. With their left hand, they would go under that leg to catch the descending ball.

Once that activity became fluid and successful, we added a second ball. Start the new exercise as before; however, with one ball in each hand, lift the right leg and toss the ball in your right hand up under your leg as before. However, as the ball is on its flight upward, quickly go around your back with the ball in your left hand, and place it in the right hand. Your empty left hand must now go quickly back to reach under your left leg to catch the descending ball.

Immediately following this goofy but profitable coordination drill, we went to our full-court dribbling drills. Each of our guards were given a tennis ball to juggle-catch with the free hand during the dribble. This kept their head up and their eyes off the basketball. The following seven drills are suggestions; however, we used these every day right through tournament play. We played jock tunes during our dribbling drills, dribbling being a rhythm activity. We executed each of the following dribble styles the length of the court two or three times. We emphasized to our players to always maintain eye contact with the approaching basket while dribbling. All of the following dribbles should be executed forcefully and quickly. The ball should have little "airtime."

1. "Slide and Glide" dribble. A useful control dribble against presses and traps. The free forearm is up to protect the dribble, in a squatting position, sliding the same foot forward while maintaining the ball position closely to the body's side. Then after two or three dribbles, reverse the ball between your legs with what we called a slam dribble (executed very inalterably) while simultaneously switching the leading forward leg and forearm.
2. Between-the-legs dribble at a fast walk. The ball is passed with each step, back to front and front to back. On all our dribble drills, we were vigilant on reminding the players to keep their eyes focused on the approaching basket.

3. Another control dribble: dribble between the legs and around the back in one motion. It is difficult to advance forward unless alternating behind the back after every other second or third between-the-leg dribble.
4. Stutter dribble with reverse dribble. The body should break down and dribble appreciatively lower during the stutter move. Do not reverse with the opposite hand. Use the same dribble hand, and keep as close to the body as possible. Opposite hand reversals are easily stripped by back-side defenders. This activity should be executed two or three times each length of the court.
5. Behind-the-body dribble. Maintain the dribble behind the back, never to dribble it in front of the body. This drill is difficult but possible. It will seem easy by the end of the first month of practices. A great dribble for fending off an unsuspecting opponent without drawing an offensive foul and successfully continuing the dribble.
6. Put-it-together dribble. All the above used with each other.
7. Speed dribble. An experienced dribbler at full-speed, out-of-control pace should be able to go the length of the gym with only four or five dribbles. Neophyte dribblers may need to use five to seven dribbles. During the speed dribble, your guards are still playing juggle-catch with a tennis ball (while incessantly mumble-griping about that requirement) in their free hand.

After the speed dribble, we quickly switched to a lay-in drill (see illustration #3) that encompassed passing only off the jump stop and receiving the pass when coming to the ball. We execute all of our perimeter passing with one hand only. The use of only the outside hand while passing keeps the ball from the opponents' reach. The follow-through on the pass looks much like the follow-through of an outside shot. Dribbling occurred only in the guard-to-guard area. Inactive players were kept to a minimum. The receiver-shooter was required to catch the ball with one hand only (one hand behind the back) and then shoot with one hand only. This taught the shooter the necessity of picking up the dribble with the outside hand maintaining control on the strong side to eliminate the ball from coming up in front of the body. Once mastered, it increases focus time and attention to the basket. We then required the receiver-shooter to go quickly around the back and fake a two-handed pass toward the opposite side of the key before the lay-in.

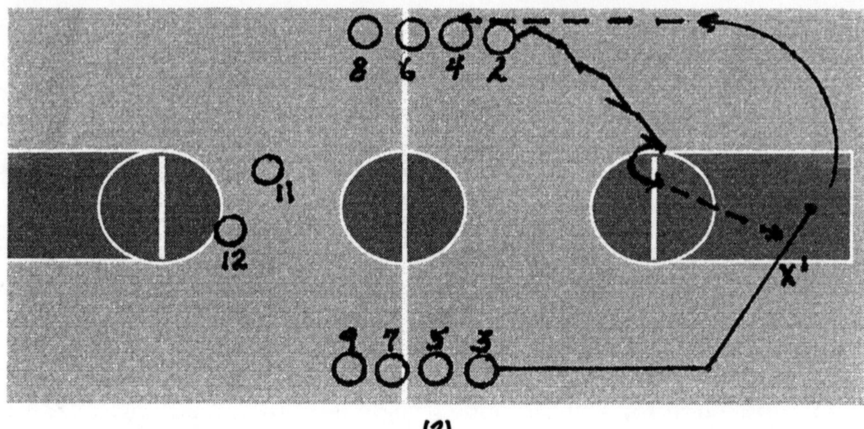

(3)

In the illustration number 3, O2 dribbles to the free-throw elbow, attacking the imagined defense and executes a reverse pivot; he then passes to O3. The timing to this lay in is the responsibility of O3. He makes an arm-over swim move and breaks to the basket at full speed when O2 starts his pivot. This shooter, as illustrated above, goes to outlet to the even-numbered sideline after the lay in, shouting out loud, "Outlet!" On receiving the outlet pass, O3 looks for O11 who has slid over to the sideline. Before the outlet pass, X1 plays passive defense on approaching player O3, making the basket attempt somewhat difficult. This defender, after making the outlet pass, then sprints out to the odd-numbered line, closing out on O5, requiring him to make a swim move before attacking the basket for his lay in pass. The passer O2 follows his pass to position himself as the new defender against O5. Players #4, #6, #8, and #10 have balls that they are pass exchanging with their even-numbered counterparts. After each pass, getting nearer to the basket. After approximately the third exchange, they will attack the defender with their turn as the players before. Players O3 and X1 have settled down to the positions that O11 and O12 occupy in the above illustration. During this lay in drill, players O11 and O12 have been waiting to finish the fast break initiated by the outlet player. O11 will attack the opposite basket with a speed dribble and gather-step-lay-in or jump-stop-fake lay in off both feet with token defensive pressure from O12. They then return to opposite ends of the lay in lines to join the alternately switching sides.

To the chagrin of the PE instructor, I marked in a spot on all the backboards for focusing and aiming at the proper contact point between ball and glass. You need a fine focus point rather than the general box area behind the rim to aim at for becoming a consistent, accurate lay-in shooter, especially when attempting lay-ins at full speed. Different approach angles cause the shooter to adjust his focus spot; however, the dot still serves a purpose. We spent much emphasis on beginning eye focus before picking up the ball. We religiously use the "Pop-Step" to begin our shooting motion. Some players can catch the ball and glide through the basket with ease without putting the ball on the floor from twenty plus feet from the basket. It was executed by leaping through the air making the catch with both feet off the floor with the right foot forward in a Nike-style-pose leap and then returning to the floor with two contacts, with the floor still in reserve. Some were particularly good at using this step to the point of using it continually. The advantage, of course, is that the player never needs to dribble. We counted out loud, celebrating made shots; we also moaned out loud on missed lay-ins. The "Pop-Step" allows focus concentration on the basket from afar due to the no need to dribble.

When defending against our lay-in drill, the receivers were required to endure much mugging from the defender or assistant coach. After the lay-in, we rebounded and stepped out-of-bounds to start the sideline break. On the receiver's sound, we passed in quickly, and the free player attacked the receiver in good close-out position. Without a sound command, the out-of-bounds ball handler slowed and controlled the toss-in.

Compose drills that are an integral part of your offense or defense. This repetitive format is necessary for consistency and game carryover. Run drills at full-speed, out-of-control pace. Even at the beginning of the season, control will follow. When a player is in a game with a full arena and his favorite cheerleader on hand and his adrenaline is gushing like Old Faithful, simple lay-ins will be missed if he has not continually practiced at that speed.

According to our aim to run drills that simulate our offense, our Hi-Post Lay-in Drill above (see illustration #4) features many of the moves, pivots, cuts, and passes that we use in our one-four high-post offense. The drill begins with four

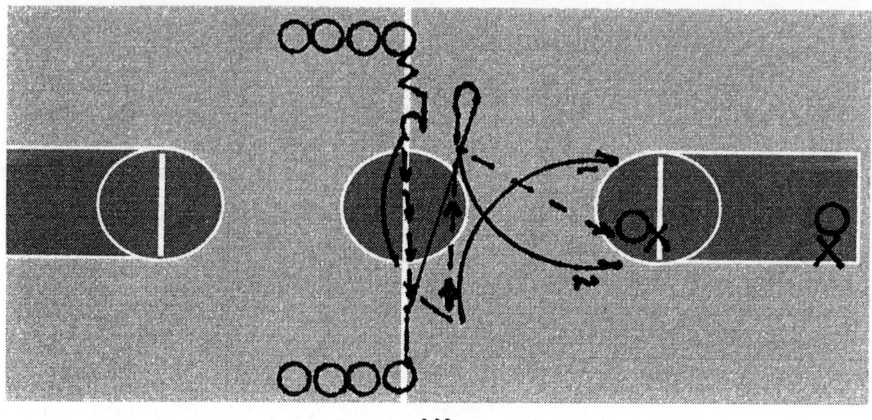

(4)

post people established permanently in the key. They alternate from offense to defense after each basket. The offensive position of the high-post player is established after a down screen from the high-post man on the run from the low-post position. As he approaches the line, he asks for the ball by lifting his outside arm, for it is on this side that a guard will come, splitting the post that receives a pass from this post man. As the post man begins the motion to pass, he nails down his inside foot and semi-pivots, stepping with his outside foot in front of his defender, toward the cutting guard, and delivers a bounce pass in front of the cutter. I am not fond of the bounce pass; it is a slower pass and not one that tall post players handle well. *(Ironically I prefer the bounce pass when a ball is being passed from around the back, for the floor converts the unusual spin of the around-the-back pass to a normal spin, which receivers are used to.)* In the case of this drill, the ball is being received by a guard who will be closely guarded in the real game. The bounce pass is thrown at the feet of the moving defender, which is physically impossible to intercept on the dead run. The post defender is semi-mauling the receiver to make the situation gamelike.

The reception of the high-post pass is completed using the block-and-snatch method. One hand is held high in front of and above the face. A pass thrown too hard will pass through two hands held up. One hand directly behind the ball will block a pass thrown too hard and fall harmlessly in front of the receiver. The snatch hand makes contact at the same time as the block hand but along the side of the ball for control.

We use four balls in this drill. The balls are in, in the case of the above illustration, the hands of the upper players. At one time during this drill, ten players are actively engaged, contrary to what the illustration shows. It begins with one of the upper players passing across the floor to the first receiver in the lower row of players. The passer follows his pass and sprints across the floor to the opposite side, passing the receiver who is dribbling towards the opposite side.

Both players come to jump stops and reverse pivot to face each other. The same action continues in the opposite direction. After the next jump stop, the passer throws a sharp pass to the post man, just establishing position at the high post. The passer follows his pass and cuts by the outside of the post receiver. The other guard cuts off the opposite side and receives the bounce pass for the lay in shot from the post man.

The shooter breaks to outlet and shouts "Outlet!" along the upper side of the court. The idle receiver at the top shouts "Ball!" to the outlet man with an arm up as a target. The other guard who cut off the post first rebounds the lay-in and makes the outlet pass. He returns to the opposite line. Both guards that split the post sprint back to their new positions in line in a closing-out defensive position, shouting "Stick, stick!" which informs his teammates that he has the ball player covered and without a dribble. This sound should eventually create a Pavlov's dog response in your players from the stimulated anticipation of a steal.

After the first two players have begun this drill, the next two players should wait until the second pass to enter the drill. Once the drill is established, three balls are being used simultaneously; and at times, twelve players are active. There is much noise. There is much movement. Fans will find it confusing to follow at first. This is good, for it makes the coach look like he has been doing something.

Keep water close on hand during practice, preferably in paper cups, which are sanitary and whose contents go down much more quickly than gimmick dispensers. Keep the cups filled so at any time, a player can splash one down, requiring minimum disruption from practice and its important flow and aerobic conditioning.

Our practices remained the same throughout the year. The repetitive nature of our drills ascertained that skill development was occurring and that game carryover was occurring. To present a player with a new physical move, like the jump stop, and practice it for a couple days, and then expect to see it used in a game situation is remotely far-fetched. It is not going to happen.

(The required need for improvement is repetition, and that is what is lacking with expensive summer basketball camps. They provide most of the scrimmage game type of situations that players enjoy; unfortunately, they avoid the more mundane but important fundamental skill-drilling activities. They focus mainly on making money, which only makes sense for a capitalistic project. I don't blame them. More often than not, summer camp graduates proudly return home with their plastic medals and trophies from camp with nothing new established in their personal basketball arsenals.)

As you learned, as a youngster in your backyard or driveway or garage, a new move had to be practiced daily, weekly, and monthly to finally master. It is the same within a team scheme. Furthermore, to be developed completely, new skills need to be encompassed in your drills and in your scrimmages for complete mastery. It is then when you will see the benefit of the repetitive method. Skill development is crucial for team success. *Tend to the incidentals, and the major things will take care of themselves.* We have all heard John Wooden of UCLA fame reiterate often that "Big things are accomplished only through the perfection of minor details." Don't worry about the players' emotional and physical needs for their full-court chaos hits. Stay with the drills; it is those activities that will provide the team with continued improvement and, as a result, a favorable win-loss record.

Our practice times get shorter and less physically intense in early February to allow worn down bodies to heal. Many factors dictate this date depending on your injuries and the nature of your injuries, also depending on your team's overall health and by the number of active players you use in a game. If you platoon substitute, your need to cut back on practice intensity and length will be much less than a team that plays only seven or eight players regularly.

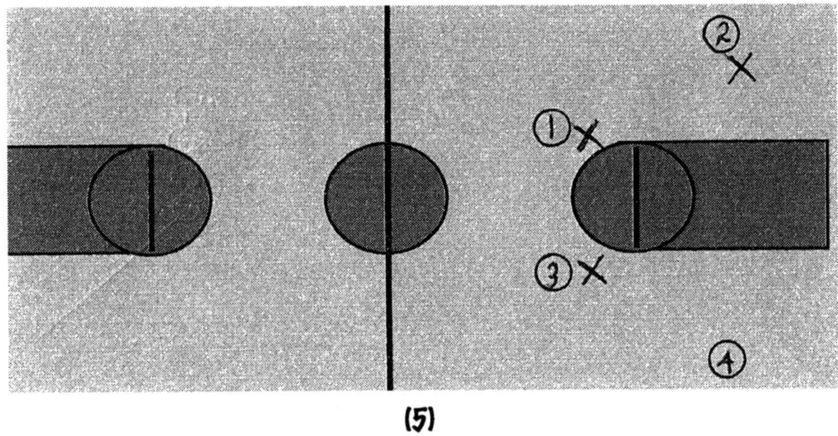

(5)

At this point in practice, we usually run our shell drill (see illustration #5). No shooting occurs. Scoring amasses from completed passes that are one-pass-away passes. One point is awarded for a completed pass to a teammate one pass away. No point or penalty for a skip pass or for a completed pass to the unguarded player. Five points per turn is a difficult score to accomplish. The practice always begins with player number 1 with the ball. Number 2 and number 3's defenders deny their opponents from the ball. If O1 passes to O4, then X3 quickly covers O4. X1 slides to guard O3. X2 slides over to guard O1. These slides continue until a pass is stolen or deflected or the defense collapses from exhaustion. Offensive players are restricted from moving (see illustration 5).

We follow the shell drill with our half-court controlled scrimmage. This is where we inserted offensive or defensive schemes. Later, at the end of practice, we would use these schemes in our full-court scrimmage or situation-ball period at full speed.

Following is our full-court lay-in drill (see illustration 6), which enforced our sideline break and had many vocal rules.

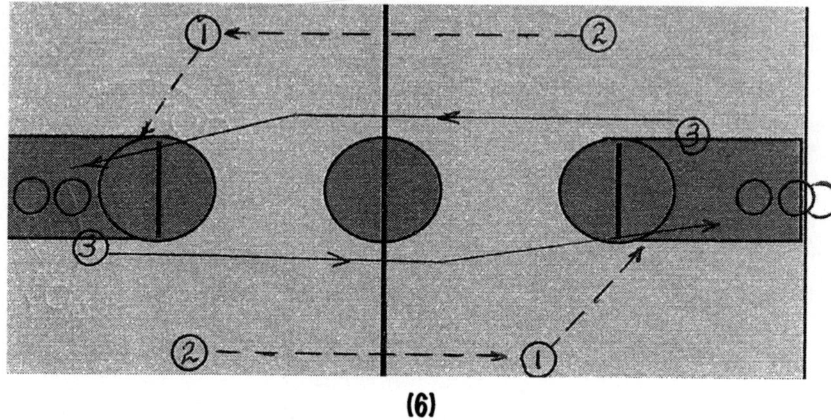

(6)

Rotations: You need two balls. Start the exercise with both O2 players holding a ball. Both O3 shooters become new opposite side outlets after the lay-in, with a resounding holler for the outlet pass. Both O2's, outlet receivers, are in the outlet receiving positions; and they pass to the O1's, and then they follow their passes to take over the positions they passed to. O1's catch the long court passes and show a diversion motion as if to shoot the three-point shot by bringing the ball and elbow up. Instead, they pass to the O3's for the "Pop Step" lay in. After the O3's complete their lay ins, they sprint to the opposite side of the court for the outlet pass, shouting, "Outlet!" Both O1's go to the end of the shooter lines. *(A variance for more increased passing, O2 can pass to O3, and then O3 passes to O1.)* It can be confusing at first, but if you just keep reminding the players to simply follow their passes and the shooters go to outlet, they will pick it up quickly. Once the drill is mastered, the following can be included:

1. Post a coach or manager near the passing lane between both O1's and O2's.
2. Require the receivers to shout "Ball!" before the pass is sent. Receivers should only shout this command when the passing lane is open and they are uncovered.
3. Now use your coaches to randomly step into the passing lane. No shout of "Ball!" should occur when the coach interferes with the passing lane.
4. O2 the passer, on reacting to the no-"Ball!" sound, should pass back to O3. O3 the eventual shooter throws to O1, who has called "Ball!" and who

should now be open. Upon receiving the ball, O1 quickly passes it back to O3 for the lay in.

This above drill is fast, involves much running and passing and catching. It simulates our sideline break and free-throw break that we use in our games. No dribbling is allowed. In our actual games, the outlet receiver reads the defense. If the opposition is in a zone, he passes the ball on command. If the opponents have manned-up, he dribble advances toward the center, reading the situation.

Six-Baskets Drill: Every sixty seconds, one player rotates clockwise to the next drill. Twelve players, given a few seconds transfer time between drills, would mean that about 15 minutes are needed for this complete drill.

Basket #1 Basket #2
O1 O2 O3

O4

Basket #6 X Basket #3
X O5

O6

O10 O7
O12 O8
Basket #5 O9
O11 O13 Basket #4

1. **Basket #1** George Mikan drill—A continuous crossover lay-in shooting drill that alternates shooting hands with each crossover. Never allow ball to touch the ground. No dribble. Emphasize never bringing the ball down below the shoulders. Left knee up, shoot, right knee up, shoot, left knee up, shoot right knee up, shoot . . .
2. **Basket #2** O3 has 60 seconds to make as many points as possible. One point for a lay in, two points for an outside shot at free-throw distance or further. O2 rebounds to assist keeping the ball alive for O3 and keeps score. Best score carries on through the year. Have a celebration each time the score is bested.

3. **Basket #3** Three-point shooting using two balls. The three-point shooter follows his shot and then throws the ball out to the waiting open man who calls "Ball!" He then follows his pass to go behind the receiver to whom he just passed to. Now he becomes an eligible shooter again and commands aloud, "Ball!" This continues for sixty seconds. The receiver comes to the pass and executes a good jump stop for balance before the three-point attempt.
4. **Basket #4** Pick and Roll with defender. Live game situation. O7 has the ball and awaits the screen from O8. The textbook reason for the screen is to create a two-on-one situation. If the screener executes the screen correctly, he has the defender on his back hip. In a real situation, O9 would have a defender on him. This would be the 1 person of the 2 on 1. Player O8 has been eliminated by the screen and is in a nondesirable follow position. Once this drill becomes second nature, the slip screen and false screen can be taught. Set up the false screen with a hand up as if calling for a pass; three or four feet before the screen contact, the screener drops back toward the basket, losing his man because of the screen misread by the defender. On the slip screen, the screener slides by the defender, after faking the screen, to screen the opposite side. All this time, the defender is trying to stop ball advance while showing a switch look yet holding the screener's cut-away shoulder in place long enough to pick up either player.
5. **Basket #5** Begin the contest known as Tips with a skip pass. The offense has thirty seconds to score as many points as possible in the time allotted. Two points for an outside shot and one point for a put-back shot. As long as the ball does not hit the ground, the offense can keep shooting, if they are getting the rebounds and can shoot without foot contact with the floor. After the first outside shot, all consequent shots must be taken while the shooter is in the air. If a shot is missed and not rebounded or the basket is made, the next attempt must follow a skip pass as if you were restarting the game. The defenders are only permitted to screen out the offense from rebounding, nothing else. After thirty seconds, the teams switch roles.
6. **Basket #6** The "Block and Snatch" catch technique is coached. After the catch, a power pivot with elevated elbows, making a figure eight motion, is monitored. To finish this drill, the player makes a power dribble toward the basket, comes to a jump stop, and then uses the crossover step to finish. The concern here is that the post people are learning to catch the ball with one hand (the block) behind the ball and the other hand (the snatch)

alongside the ball. The purpose for the one-handed block is to eliminate those fumbles that occur when a hard pass goes between both hands. With the block-style reception, the ball is stopped; if mishandled, it will fall harmlessly and can be regathered. Regards the crossover step: When the defense is not crowding you, lift the ball, elbow high for protection, high as if in your shooting motion, and then—with a quick high ball reversal—use a crossover step with a quick power move to the basket. If the opponent is crowding you defensively, reverse pivot, and then cross over to the basket with no dribble.

The Chair Drill we run just before our full-court three-on-three drill.

(7)

We spend ten to fifteen minutes playing one-on-one full court, with the defender carrying a folding chair on his back (see news photo #7). The back of the chair would be behind the defender's head, with his wrists beside his ears holding the seat section of the chair. The defender becomes accustomed to playing defense without hands. It deterred all the silly reaching that keeps referees their jobs. It also placed much focus on balance and footwork. Our goal from the defender, within one length of the court, was to create two to three crossovers by the dribbler. In the introductory phase of this drill, the dribblers were asked to play three-fourth speed and to be in charge of control, no crashes. Once a team couple had navigated the length of the gym down and back, the roles changed and they swapped the chair. This is a very exhausting drill.

While coaching the Chair Drill, the coaching staff emphasized to all defenders to *stay in front of the ball not the man dribbling the ball*. This forces crossovers and makes it harder for the dribbler to beat the defender. Once you begin guarding the man instead of the ball, you have converted to a chasing position on the opponent's first dribble. Don't give the ball handler an advantage to the left because he is right-handed. What will happen? You are going to get beat to the left. Jeez!

One of my favorite ball-handling passing-receiving drills was what we called the two-by-two by two-by-two (if you have an assistant with a speech impediment do not embarrass him—you call out the drill). This drill quickly demonstrates who your less accomplished ball handlers are. Uncontested turnovers, not unlike cigarette lites, are nails to the coffin of a basketball coach. They act on a coach exponentially. The more uncontested the turnover, the more severe their affect. The more important a game, the more the uncontested turnover hammers the coach psychologically and physiologically. These turnovers have more influence on a coach's coaching longevity than exercise, nutrition, genetics, or dark chocolate. The two-by-two drill creates uncontested turnovers; it exudes these turnovers. As a coach, you should be careful of prolonged exposure during this exercise. I believe I could have coached another twenty years if it hadn't been for this debacle of a drill. This two-by-two drill pits two of your offensive players, preferably ball handlers, against eight defenders. These defenders have separate zones that they are responsible for. They cannot leave these areas. An exception is they are not limited in space laterally. So they may double up with their partner to the side. Your guards must navigate this maze with a dribble limitation. After each catch they are allowed two dribbles. This drill demands much pressure on the open man to find passing lanes or open gaps. The ball handler's pressure is obvious. The offense must go down and back without a mistake. An error stops their advancement; it is at this point where they must start over. About the second month, we allow no dribbles. This drill is not a panacea to what ails your team with poor passing problems, but it is a good start.

Luck is the product of when preparation meets opportunity. You can't control opportunities, but you can prepare for those free possessions by practicing for them. Set up drills that encourage scrambling for the ball. Demand the continuance of this scrambling aggression in your other drills. Practice and set up drills for breaking shyness from contact. Kneepads will make a perceivable difference in loose-ball aggression. One of our drills had three players in the key area. A coach would toss in a rolling ball. We would expect to see nothing but a—holes and elbows. Because of the stalwart efforts needed to succeed in this drill, the winning players were rewarded intrinsically. This drill at times became quite frenzied. Grabbing and holding are allowed in these drills. We never worried about the carryover game effect. Besides, my experience in these habits is that it is easier to rein back aggression than it is to increase it later in the season. Besides, referees are very lenient on contact during scrambles for a loose ball. This is a good time to warn your players of the physical tricks that might be employed by your opponents in close physical play such as jersey grabbing to pull the opponent over on yourself for drawing a foul. Following this scramble work, we normally went to the next two following drills. The three-lane-rush for passing practice and then to the UCLA drill for a controlled scrimmage simulation encompassing the prior techniques just used. *With all our fast-break work, we emphasized playing quick and fast but not rushing our play.*

The three-lane full-court rush was a full-speed exercise down and back without a dribble. The players were allowed only three passes; the last pass, before the lay-in came off of a jump stop. If the ball touched the floor for any reason, such as after the made lay in, the three executing the rush would do it over. The lay-in had to be successful. They continued to execute it down and back without a mistake. A favorite coach's diatribe often heard and echoed during this drill was, "Make it easy on yourself!"

The following (see illustration 8) is called the UCLA drill. This is a three-on-two continuation and transition full-court drill with a chaser making it a three-on-three.

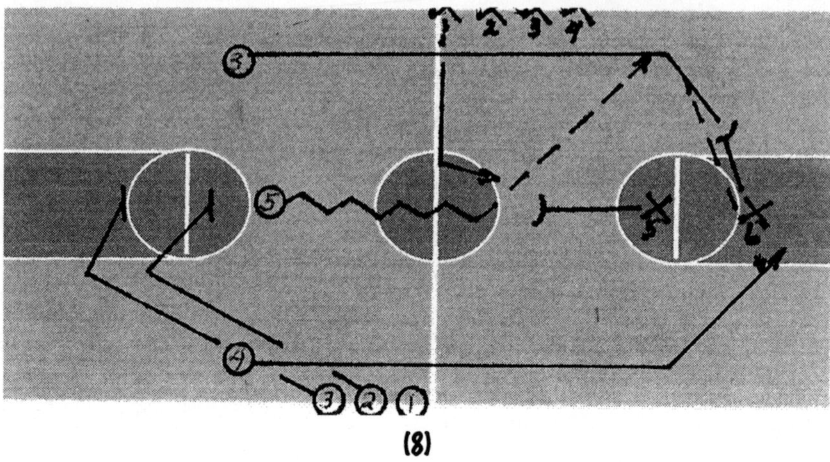

(8)

Once the ball crosses the midcourt line, X1 sprints in and touches the midcourt center circle. He then goes in pursuit of the O's to help his defenders. Also, once the offense crosses the midcourt line, the substitutes O3 and O2 go onto the court to the opposite end to set up their tandem defense to defend the X's who will be returning once the shot has occurred at the opposite end of the court. Like the earlier rotation, once the X's have crossed the midcourt line, O1 enters to touch the midcourt center circle and then pursues the action. Once a team attempts or makes a shot, they return to the sideline to get ready to come in again. The chaser coming in behind the three-on-two situation gives a feeling of a gamelike fast break. O5 should not pass the ball until he makes X5 commit to him. Only one shot is allowed per team. No put backs. The emphasis here is fast transition from defense to break to offense.

We tried to run the above drills at every practice. We believed they encompassed all the skills necessary to run our defenses and offenses. We believed enough in these exercises that we seldom varied them. We always finished our practices with a scrimmage and situation play and then our shoot-to-leave free-throw drill.

Our coaches would demonstrate how a three-on-one fast break can be enhanced by dropping an offensive player to create a two-on-one break. Try it in a controlled situation. It is easier to score with two-on-one. Your passing lanes become wider and harder to cover. We showed this for philosophical knowledge. We never coached or expected this type of transition, because at the high school level, we worried about their leadership abilities. At full speed, I could imagine this decision-making process. It would likely produce all three deciding to drop back at the same time, leaving us with no shooter . . .

(9)

To simulate game-type tension, competition, and pressure on free-throw shooting, we kept a "ladder" (see photo right) on our players' individual daily practice shooting percentages. We shot the "ladder" at a different time at each practice. The free-throw ladder was a piece of three-fourths plywood, 6 × 18 inches, with a hole cut out of it for a handle (see photo #9). I had twelve hooks in single file screwed into it. One-inch circular tags hung from the hooks. Each tag had a player's name on it. They were color coded for instant recognition. Every other hook had a star next to it. The top position on the ladder was coveted. Each day's contests over ladder movement were taken very seriously by our players. Off and on, I would hang the ladder in the school for all to see. On the opening day of practice, I threw all the labeled tags into a hat. In the order each player picked up a tag, he hung that tag from the highest available hook. This was fun; much celebrating and moaning accompanied each draw and placement. In over thirty years of coaching, only twice did I see the first picker pick his own name. Boy, did that create some contesters. Once, I saw a player place his tag on the bottom hook. I loved his arrogance, truly captain stock, and it took him only a few weeks to eventually claim the first position.

On even days, tags hanging from the starred hooks challenge the tag above them. On odd days, the tags hanging from the blank hooks challenge upward. Only the challengers, if successful, could move their tag upward. If their challenge failed, both tags stayed where they were until the next day's challenges. The challenge was the best of twenty attempts. Only two shots at a time could be taken. Between shooting turns, each player had to sprint dribble the length of the gym while his challenger shot. This maintained a fast heartbeat and a gamelike shooting experience. Both shooters could orally interfere with the other; they were not permitted to make any physical contact with each other during the shot attempt. This screaming and badgering created some further gamelike tension. Much imaginative "smack talking" was developed during these challenges. On missed attempts, once the shooter returned from his run, he had to do ten fingertip push-ups.

The top tags were always my free-throw shooters for a game technical. When a technical was called, I merely yelled out to the team, "Who is higher among you on the ladder?" They always knew. When a player was absent, the challenges continued. If you were above an absent challenger, you needed to make at least 12 of your 20 attempted shots to maintain your ladder position. Conversely, if you were challenging an absent player, you could pass him by making twelve completions. On challenges that ended in a tie, we had shootouts. Each of the two players had two shots to break the tie. They kept alternating turns until a winner evolved. Earlier rules applied. All team members gathered for the shoot offs. The coaches divided the team into two supporting groups, one for each shooter. The jeering and harassing was always loud and supportive. This was one of the few times many players stood around inactively during our practices. It was worth it; these periods became intense, and the players seemed to have fun with the drill.

At the end of the season, for the awards banquet, I would go to a secondhand store and pick up an old folding ladder. I would present it to the player who ended at the top of the ladder on our last practice. The losing players and their parents reveled in watching someone else win this award and the nuisance and inconvenience that accompanied it. Our last free-throw challenge vignette must have seemed somewhat curious to the observer. The last challenge between the ladder's numbers one and two appeared passive and nonaggressive and vitiated the intent.

At the end of every practice, our team lined up behind the free-throw line. A player was eligible to go home if he hit his free throw and the player behind him shot successfully. If not, both went back to the end of the line to await their next turns. Only the shooter who made his shot was eligible to go home, but before he did, he had to go quickly to a free-throw sideline position with both hands held high. If he didn't assume this position before his teammate shot, he lost his opportunity to go home even if that player made his shot. Our overall game free-throw shooting statistics were normally higher than our opponents.

Free-Throw Shooting Tips

1. Call your free throws free points, for that's what they should be.
2. Remind your shooters of the short distance—less than 14 feet once the arm is extended over the 15-foot line. (This distance was established in the 1894-95 season.)
3. Impress your players of the basket ring circumference by demonstrating how three girls' basketballs will go through at the same time. It takes very little pressure to push them through. Very impressive. Another graphic illustration of the small size of the ball relative to the rim circumference is to have each player lie directly under the basket to watch a boy's ball go through when it doesn't touch the rim. The difference in size becomes very obvious.
4. Place the ball onto your hand, palm up, and move your hand in a sweeping motion. The grip used to control the ball from falling out is about the same grip tightness you should use for holding the ball during the shot.
5. The shooting index finger tip should be in line with the ball valve and in a ball groove. The guide hand should be alongside the ball but not providing any force.
6. The shooting elbow should be above the same side knee that is a few inches ahead of the other foot. Avoid a perfect perpendicular stance to the basket. A right-handed shooter's toes should be pointed slightly to the left. This enables the shooting elbow to be in a comfortable perpendicular position to the basket.
7. The shot release should occur once the shooting elbow rises above the eyebrows. *Both elbow and wrist should snap at the same time* on the release of the ball. The follow through should cause the shooter's fingertips to vibrate after release of the ball. The outstretched hand should be pronated, with the index and middle fingers still visibly pointed down through the basket until the ball nears the rim. The feet should still be rising, fully extended on the toes or even at a fraction of an inch off the floor surface.

8. Find a comfortable rhythm, and stay with it. Don't rush the shot. Before you shoot, see it go through in your mind. Make certain that all physical actions are directly in line with the basket.

Before or after situation play, we scrimmaged (hallelujah!). No matter how tired our players were, they were always up for scrimmaging. We either began or ended practice with situation play, which was another favorite period of practice. Situation play is scrimmaging under given limits, under a given game situation. An example of situation play: Tell the teams there is one minute left in the game. One of the teams is down by one point (don't tell your two teams who is behind, who has possession, and who is leading until just before time-out is called). Both teams are in the bonus. The team in possession has one of their players with four fouls, and one of the opposition cannot convert at the charity line, and you have two time-outs. The opposition will have similar scenarios to consider. The coaches began each situation with a shortened twenty-second time-out for both teams to devise plans. We shortened the time-out periods to allow for more situations in our given practice time. It was thought by shortening these periods, communicating would be more intense, thus honing our players' listening skills. In a real game situation, their short time-out periods would seem extended. In these time-outs, the coaches would remind the teams to devise a plan B in case their initial plans failed or changed.

To bring attention to our upcoming season, to hedge on the opening day by beginning a minute after midnight, to bring excitement over opening day, and for creating team and fan unity, we engaged in "Midnight Madness"—I'm sure an evening celebrated in hundreds of high schools across our nation. We included in this collage of basketball nonsense "Dads' Night Out," which invited our players' fathers to spend the night with the team in the gym. We suggested that they bring their sleeping bags. No-stake poker games were organized, basketball videos were played. Father-son team shooting competitions were organized, and winners received Starbucks gift cards. A few minutes before the witching hour, coaches would give spine-tingling pep talks, and then at midnight, the varsity team aspirants would run on the floor to do a few, rehearsed, and coached lay in drills. After an hour of organized practice, the fans were excused, and the players and their dads returned to continue the revelry of Dads' Night Out.

In our state, basketball season used to always start on November 1. This date made it ideal for Midnight Madness. Halloween party treats were in order. Our players were off the streets on Halloween as high school age players should be. The holiday seemed to make the evening more festive. Now the state elects to begin the winter sports date by the shape of the moon?

To further celebrate the start of basketball, we would encourage students and fans to bring toilet paper rolls to the first game. On the occurrence of our first made basket, everyone would hurl their toilet rolls across the gym. Before the contest began, we would inform the referees of this tradition. We also told them that there would be very little delay of the game; everyone in the gym was prompted to pull in their rolls or help pick them up. To my surprise, the referees always agreed to this malarkey. However, opposing coaches seldom saw the point of reason. Also, our school custodians were always upset over the missing toilet paper rolls from their facilities. I imagine there were also a few fans that became discomforted over the missing conveniences. We quit this TP celebration. However, I recommend it; Just first take the time to solve the custodians' concerns. I have to say the crisscrossing of streamers was quite a scene. A floating tissue paper rendition of a massive spider web hanging over the floor for a quick "moment in time." (See photo below.) It is a memory that will always stay fond to me. You may want to stay with something simple like a standing applause?

Fans and players cleaning up the floor. Referee looks a little confused.

Some important practice tips worth rementioning:

1. Be organized.
2. Keep drills related to your offense and your defense.
3. Work your players extremely hard, and keep your practices active.
4. Allow your players to laugh; assure them that the practices are hard but fun.
5. Make your practices gamelike.
6. Provide extra time for repetition of drills and techniques.
7. Make everything competitive. Keep score on everything competitive.
8. Demand discipline, timeliness, technique, and respect.
9. Treat all members of the team as family.

Chapter 4

Soft Presses

I coached at a small school that was limited in talent and numbers. Year after year, we won or were runners-up in our competitive league. We contributed our success to variations of the soft press.

There are times when a coach feels that his or her team can secure a victory by merely trading shots with an opponent. More often than not, coaches must call on alternative methods to secure a victory. When your team is not as gifted in shooting as your opponents and are without any height advantages or are less athletic and/or, heaven forbid, slower than your opponents, then alternative methods are necessary to become and stay competitive. One good alternative method is the soft press. The term soft press means that the defense is not going to cover the opponent on the inbound pass, nor is it going to confront them for turnovers immediately after the toss-in. Soft presses, as opposed to full-court presses, when played with sound discipline and proper rotation, are not as chancy or reckless.

By concentrating the action to midcourt, your opponent's shooting abilities are limited; their height advantage is nullified, becoming a hindrance, and your team might begin controlling the game tempo, which is an unnerving situation for teams that are used to being in control. Speed is the opponent's remaining advantage, as it is always; but by good positioning and clever anticipatory play, that too can somewhat be harnessed.

Two simple but effective soft presses are the 221 half-court press and the 131 half-court press. Your personnel's talent and the opponent's press-breaking methods will dictate which of the two to use. Presses create extra pressure, pressure that builds over the length of a game. Opponents will seem to have more difficulty in beating your press in the second half of the game due to the exponential and exhausting effects of the pressure. A good dictator of the effect of the soft press is by how many uncontested breakaway lay-ins opponents have scored against your soft press. At halftime, if your stats show only one or two of these lay-ins, your team is probably not gambling enough on steal attempts. Conversely, if the opponent is garnering too many breakaway lay-ins, then you probably need to look at tempering your pressure or adjusting your defensive rotations. Recognizing that zone presses encourage passing, thus speeding up the flow of the game; it is necessary for you to practice regularly at this tempo, whereby you create an advantage over opponents that practice at a less controlled pace. If your opponents use similar pressing game tactics, so be it, then your team should react more favorably to their pressure.

Roles (Initial Player Positioning)

Teams are inclined to favor one side of the court when attacking presses, normally the right side. We have optimized our talent at those positions that defend the best against a right-sided attack. So we are also inclined to force early action to that side. We practice to prepare for either attack side.

Player #1 should be a player that sees the floor well and is not shy of eye-to-eye contact *(see illustration 10)*. This defender should keep an eye on the ball handler's eyes. If the ball handler is looking to pass down floor, then additional pressure is needed to bring their attention back to the dribble. The role of this defender is to guide the ball handler to the midcourt line along the sideline without allowing a short penetrating pass or reversal pass. The trap should occur at the half court, along the sideline, with the assistance of player #3. Player #1 should close out, unlike the close out on a shot, but with both arms down and wide, encouraging the ball carrier to pass sideways or backward. Arms down allows better continued man-to-man coverage if the ball handler is still dribbling.

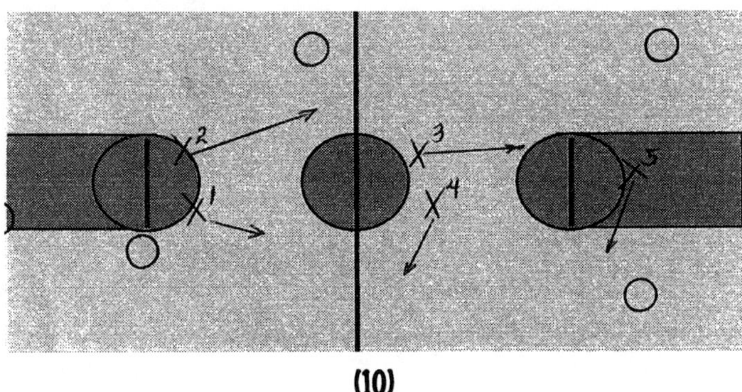

(10)

Player #2 should be one of your quickest players; a shoplifting record is not detrimental. This player is to first deter the inbounds pass to his side, not necessarily in an attempt to steal it, albeit you would accept that turnover. Once player #1 has control of the ball handler, then player #2 fades back to a position we call center field and anticipates the opponent who is most likely to receive the pass from the upcoming trap. The backcourt pass is not as important a release to cover as a pass behind #2's position. If you were to shift to the 131 soft press, this player would move to the center position, which is a simple shift, all other roles remaining the same.

Player #4 can be your slowest player on the floor who doesn't shy from contact and one who understands "Stand Still." The role of player #4 is to stop the dribble advance, to take a charge, and/or to assist on the midcourt trap with both hands held high to force a steal-able lob pass for player #5, who I will introduce later.

Player #3 should be tall, can be slow, and should be adept at stopping one-on-one situations under the basket. This position is extremely enhanced with a player gifted at taking charges, for this occurs often at this position. The role of player #3 is to read the press break direction. If the ball movement is coming down the opposite side of the court then player #3 must rotate back to #5's position, which is at center court under the opponent's basket.

Player #5 should be quick and will wager on anything. The role of player #5 is to steal long passes into the key area, to take charges on coast-to-coast drivers, and to steal the lob pass over the trap at the midcourt corner. The highest amount of passes out of the trap will occur down the strong side sideline.

Rules

All defensive players should initially position themselves to encourage long steal-able passes and do not allow the ball to be brought or thrown down the middle of the court. Players #1 and #2 should line up with their backs close to each other, making an offensive split entry difficult. If the opponent does split your primary defenders, everyone should immediately drop back to a half-court defense.

Considering the above setup, if player #2 can deny the inbounds pass to his or her side, all the better—for you can then use the strengths of your initial setup and its respective personnel assets. Once entry has been made, hopefully to the left side of the court, player #1 should force the ball handler to continue the dribble down that side with token pressure, guiding the dribbler to the trap area. Player #4 needs to assist in that endeavor by staying back from trapping the dribbler until that time to trap. A workable rule has been that player #4 should mirror-reflect the ball handler in position and depth from the midcourt line, shading a foot or two to the inside, beginning once the ball handler has reached a point 20 feet or more from the midcourt, adjusting of course for the ball handler's speed and intention. That position should coincide when player #4 recognizes that the stop can be made at the midcourt line with just enough time to get to the sideline with the outside foot out-of-bounds. The out-of-bounds foot placement by the outside trapper is very important, although slightly illegal? *(See illustration 11.)*

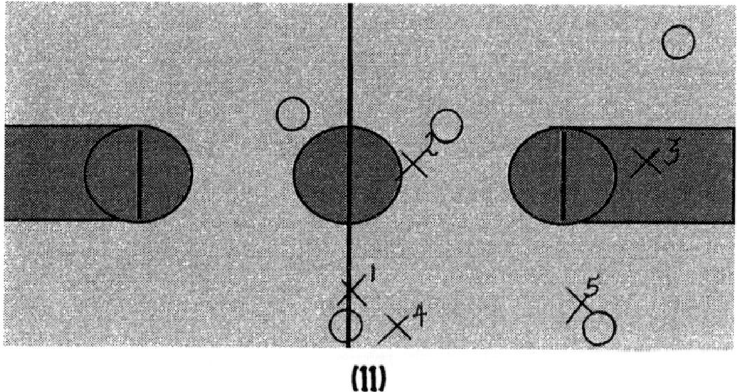

(11)

The trap should occur between the #1 and #4 players, and ideally, it should occur on or near the midcourt line along the sideline, which acts as a sixth player. This location presents the ball handler with stressful decision making, such as "Has the ten-second backcourt count expired?" "Am I violating the over-and-back rule?" and if not, "Where is the referee on the five-second over-guarding count?" All these plus the pressure of the sideline trap while looking for receivers. The remaining offensive players, except for the furthest diagonally cross-court receiver, should be covered in a smothering man-to-man deny stance.

Rotations

By the first rotation, you have successfully divided the court and denied any comfortable close passes; with two defenders trapping the same individual, your science majors will quickly pick up someone who will be uncovered. That opening should be the furthest diagonally away offensive player. (See illustration 12.) Should the opponent's guards reverse the ball between each other, your trappers merely trade roles. Your deep court protector must shift from protecting under the basket to assisting the trapper with the new trap location. Ideally, this should occur at or before midcourt to as deep as the free-throw line extended. Once that line is crossed, I personally discourage further trapping because the base line coming up acts as an additional defensive player. Obviously, this soft press with its shortened passing lanes is only as strong as the pressure that your first trappers inflict on the ball handler.

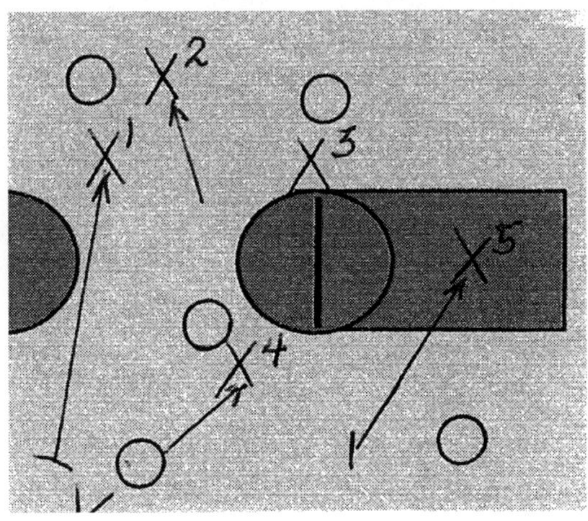

(12)

Coaching Tips

1. Don't give up early on the press. Sometimes, the soft press will seem to be just an annoyance to the opponents. Later in the game, under the same conditions and format, it may create complete chaos for the opponent; besides being physiologically sensible, it sends a nonverbal message to your opponents and to your own players.
3. Work a lot on taking various forms of charges.
4. Keep your players from locking their knees on trapping positions. Most players tend to try to enlarge their bodies on traps, and this is difficult to coach out of them. Not only should their trapping movements be fast and disruptive but loud and wet.
5. Coach the 131 soft press along with your 221 soft press. In a contest where the opponents call time-out, they are going to use that time discussing how to set up an offensive receiver in the center of your 221 soft press or a receiver back a few yards from your initial trap. What to their surprise when taking the court to meet your 131 soft press with a center defender right where they set up their receiver. They have wasted a time-out! *Chuckle.*
6. On free throw attempts by the opponents, keep your #5 man down floor rather than under the basket for the free-throw rebound. The odds are good the basket will be made, and player #5 won't be needed for the rebound and will better serve you in a down-court ready position for the soft press. Spend a good amount of time on your players sprinting to their help defensive positions should the trap be split or broken.

131 Soft Press

The 131 soft press is a mutated clone of the 221 press. Easy to coach if you are already using the soft 221 press. A good alternative press with all the tools of the 221 press. The 131 press is essentially the 221 soft press after the initial rotation of player #2 toward the center court. A preferable press to the 221 press for the team with less overall quickness. My reluctance to begin the game with this press is that it is not as daring and challenging as the wider set of the 221 press. The positive feature of the established center fielder, generally my position #2 player, hinders the opponent's use of a center-oriented press break. It also establishes defensive center control without your #2 player having to defend this coverage area on the sprint from the sidelines. The established centerfield feature of the 131 soft press provides an ideal position for optimizing the skills of a gifted defensive player. Being the preferred press of a slower team, its conservative nature compared to the 221 soft press reduces the easy successful break.

Roles

Player #1 should be a player that sees the floor well, and like the 221 press, this player is not timid about entering new relationships. Close contact and traffic control are two personal bullets on this player's resume. He is required to coerce the opponent's dribbler into falling into a midcourt sideline-corner trap. The defensive control by this player should be nonthreatening so that there are no pass reversals. Monitoring the dribbler's eyes is important. If the dribbler seems to be looking for someone to pass to, a more aggressive defensive stance will avert his attention back to the dribble.

Player #2 should anticipate well. Any prophetic skills would be a big bonus for this player. I recommend your best defensive player placed in this area. There is much area to defend; however, more passes occur. Thus, more steal attempts come through this area than elsewhere on the press. Much emphasis must be placed on instructing this player to imagine his head on a swivel. The coverage area behind him toward the opposition's basket is first priority. If there is no receiver behind him, he has carte blanche over all parts of the court to terrorize.

Player #3 has the same duties as player #4, although mirrored. Because of the opponent's inclination for bringing the ball down the right side, Player #4 should be the better trapper of the two.

Player #4, as in the 221 soft press, can still be your slowest player on the floor. The request to take charges should generate a twinkle in his eye. His ability to trap and maintain footwork balance is important. When the trap occurs on the opposite side of the floor, which it often does, his nature should be that of a

German Shepherd, very protective. He will often be called to rotate under the basket as the last line of defense.

Player #5 should be quick and will be called on to make the steal, which occurs often, from the pass of the trapped dribbler, which will be lobbed over trapper #3 or #4 depending on the side of the court. Player #5 will often be given the opportunity for stealing long coast-to-coast passes. To prepare this player for those steals, you should practice long tosses into his area so he becomes intuitive about what passes are steal-able.

Rules

On the initial toss-in, all defensive players should sell their positions as being receptive to the long pass. This first line of defense is important because this steal attempt draws no one from their assigned positions. To eliminate the early leg flex needed for making the first step, we require our players to maintain that position by constantly being in the athlete's position. Quickness advantage with the first defensive step is improved. It is necessary to bend at the knee before the explosive extension of the first step. This time taken to flex down should be eliminated. All players should shade their respective opponent to encourage the first entry pass to be made toward a desired side—the side that you have optimized with your personnel's individual talents.

The trap should occur between the #1 player and either players #3 or #4; and ideally, as in the soft 221 press, it should occur on or near the midcourt line along the sideline which acts as a sixth player. This location presents the ball handler with stressful decision making such as, 'Has the ten-second backcourt count expired, am I violating the over and back rule and if not where is the referee on the five-second over-guarding count?' All this plus the pressure of the sideline trap while looking for receivers. The remaining offensive players, except for the furthest diagonally cross court receiver, should be covered in a smothering man-to-man deny stance.

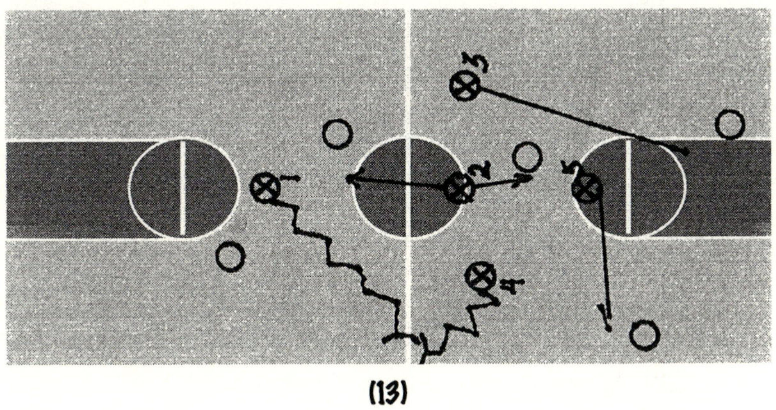

(13)

Rotations

Once the oppositions guard has ball control, player #1 forces him to the trap area with token pressure. (see illustration 13) Just enough pressure to maintain proper direction without duress. Players #3 and #4 need to assist in that endeavor by staying back from trapping the dribbler until that time to trap. A workable rule has been that player #3 or #4, depending on what side the ball is on, should mirror reflect the ball-handler in position and depth from the midcourt line, shading a foot or two to the inside, beginning once the ball handler has reached a point 20 feet or more from the midcourt, adjusting—of course—for the ball handler's speed and intention. That position should coincide when player #3 or #4 recognizes that the stop can be made at the midcourt line with just enough time to get to the sideline with the outside foot out-of-bounds. Once it is apparent which side the ball will cross, the opposite trapper, #3 or #4, must rotate back towards the free throw area. Player #5 has started rotating up to the strong side in anticipation of the lob pass over the trap along the sideline.

If the ball penetrates the free-throw line extended, further pressing or trapping is up to the coach. In the 221 press, the slides and helps necessary to continue further pressing become complicated. In the 131 soft press, the confusion is less when converting to a half-court 131 zone defense. The most difficult rotation to coach is teaching all players how to collapse to the key area once the press is broken. Your trailers are the most difficult, for they tend to feel excused when passed by; just the opposite, they need to chase as if they were alongside the ball handler. A good drill for combating this situation is the UCLA Drill. (See page 60, illustration 8)

Coaching Tips

1. Keep an eye on player #1 for tiring. This press is exhausting for #1 with the double duty of chasing the ball against a two-man front in the backcourt and trying to force play to a particular place.
2. Have a few trapping drills, and practice them regularly.
3. On free-throw attempts by the opponents, keep your #5 man down floor rather than under the basket for the free-throw rebound. The odds are good the basket will be made, and player #5 won't be needed for the rebound and will better serve you in a down-court ready position for the soft press.
4. Spend a good amount of time on your players sprinting to their help defensive positions should the trap be split or broken.
5. This press is only as good as the first trap. Make certain that your players have no inhibitions about waving and shouting frantically while trapping. While frantic shouting may contribute to vulgar expectorating, it certainly won't hurt your cause. Yuk!

To break the 131 Trap, screen the middle defender. Spread your guards before crossing the midcourt, working the middle defender to create gaps to dribble attack, point, or post up your post person 10 feet behind the trap, all while attacking those gaps.

A sidebar:

Another interesting even press (*two up front*) was championed to me by Jimmy Anderson, long time assistant coach and head coach of the Oregon State Beavers. During his assistantship with Hall of Fame coach Ralph Miller, he developed and tweaked a 2-1-2 hard press. Then maybe even more difficult, he sold Coach Miller on using it. The up-two defenders played a deny-type defense, forcing the inbounds passer to alley-oop his entry pass. The #1 player would attempt to steal that pass or harass the receiver. From the press, they dropped back to a three-two match-up zone. If the point was to dribble the ball to the wing, the point defender would match up and follow the dribble. The wing defender would slide behind the couple and take the abandoned position at the top.

I said earlier to not give up on the press. There are times it will not click. These times are normally early in the game, and you will question yourself why you are still in it. Play it softer, but don't quit on it. Perhaps this is the best time of all to continue it. You can analyze it and possibly tweak it and improve it. The message to your team when you drop the press during a game is certainly not the reinforcement they need at that time. I am a complete believer in defensive pressure, especially in the latter part of the game and especially at the high school level. These are kids making decisions on the floor. Stir in pressure and what seems as simple on the court as the simple task of spelling cat, will not get by C or A.

Chapter 5

Zone Defenses and Man-to-Man Defenses

To the basketball purist, any defense but man-to-man is gimmickry. One who recognizes the affront of this statement is the coach who teaches and uses zone defenses. Half-court zones were designed to combat teams that shoot like they could not hit open space from a satellite, for teams who struggle with patience, for poor passing teams, and for teams with distinct height advantages and their resultant mismatches. A residual use of the half-court zone is the ability to hide a defender who is in foul trouble.

The strength of a zone defense comes from its numbers in or close to the key area. Zone defenses are extremely difficult to coach. They maintain tight containment while adjusting the need for choreographed movements, rotations and slides, while continuing to optimize your personnel strengths. To maintain all the objectives of a zone defense is extremely challenging to coach. The 131 zone in its original look is less seen than other popular zones, thus is unfamiliar to most opponents. Most zones will have practically the same adjusted position alignments after the first entry pass or wing pass. It is the original setup of the 131 zone that converts readily to the fast break; it also presents high pressure against a perimeter-oriented offense and defensively converts easily between high-post and low-post offenses. As a team, any zone should attempt to organize its position high. Many teams compensate against this strategy by running their zone offense higher than practical, albeit unconsciously. Most coaches and players cringe when they see a zone defense. Coaches worry about their team's ability to shoot well from the outside, and their players resent the consequent lack of opportunities for "shaking and baking" moves, which are—unfortunately—normally dear to the hearts of offensive players.

Roles (Initial Player Positioning)

Player #5, who we call Rover, is in the best position to see the offensive plays and sets. (See illustration 14.) The Rover has the best visual seat on the floor of the opponent's offense. Thus he or she should be your defensive quarterback and should call your zone adjustments. A player with a positive grade point average, in their core classes, would be a wise choice. The Rover will be called upon to defend from baseline corner to baseline corner depending on the wing's defensive instructions. Initial positioning should be somewhat vertical to the ball. When sandwiching the low-post player, your Rover should be the outside slice of the sandwich.

Players #3 and **#2** ideally are your best pass anticipators and should be fast. Good one-on-one pressure instincts are needed for the traps that your 131 defense will present. Personally, my teams only trapped on the perimeter after the ball has penetrated the free-throw line extended. These players must cover between three-point shooting and the higher inside shooting areas plus low-post coverage on the weak side of the zone defense. The defensive abilities of your individual wings will constitute their consequent coverage boundaries. We constantly reminded our wings how important their coverage areas were. Without constant sprint coverage, shooters were going to get set shots. It is necessary to watch for tiring from your wings, for late in the game, they must continue to sprint cover. Remember Murphy's law on last-second shooters, "Leave them open, and they all become money."

Player #1 must be able to play tirelessly. #1 will be called on to switch zone principles with man-to-man coverage depending on the offensive situations. Player #1 will be called upon to guard the perimeter and/or to assist with the high-post area depending on whether you are playing a soft 131 or a hard 131. *This will be explained later under rules.*

Player #4, who we have always affectionately called Chubby, is ideally tall and is relegated to the key area and is not allowed to leave it. He/she is your true zone player. Against low-post players, Chubby plays the inside slice of the sandwich (Diagram 2). Any pistol defense relegates him to the bench. Chubby must play with his or her head on a swivel and deny post flashes. You cannot do that in the old cowboy "pistols" one-on-one stance.

Rules

All defensive players must assist by packing the paint for deterring the first pass from going to a low-post player. When teams post two low receivers in the key, this initial alignment without wide-armed defensive coverage is vulnerable to penetrating passes. However, this possible weakness can also be exploited to your advantage by the baiting of poor judgment passes by your Rover. Once a pass has been made to a wing player, your defensive weak-side player must rotate to a position under the basket, in front of the rim. Your players must know that the 131 defense is also susceptible at the high-post elbows. All defenders must always keep their arms up high and wide. Upon reaching the midcourt line, before setting up in their zone positions, your players should be running backwards.

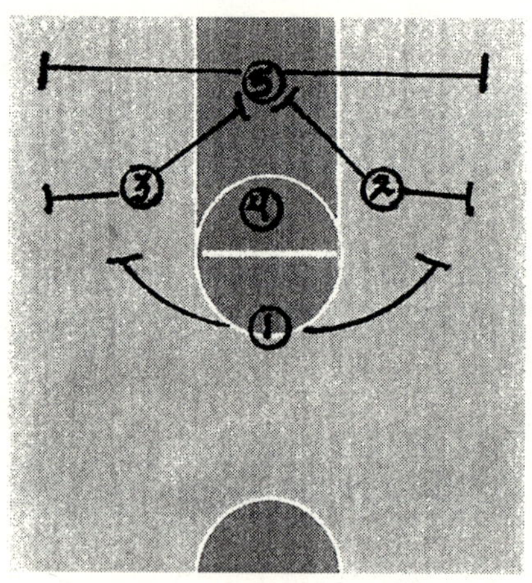

(14)

Defensive stances, other than post people, are the same stances you would coach using man-to-man principles. Post defenders are taught to keep one hand on the back side of the strong side shoulder of the offensive post man, generally the opposite shoulder that the post man is signaling for the ball. On reception by the post, this pressure on his shoulder will deter his motion to the basket or from hooking the defensive player.

Rotations

On a pass by the offense to the wing, the rover must swing to that side to front post people or assist the wing man with a trap, if the ball has passed the block. Chubby should shift to the free-throw line above the block. Your weak-side wing rotates to a position under the basket. Your point person will assist with post coverage or deny the pass back to the point area. In hard coverage, your point defender plays man-to-man on the ball or on the closest offensive player to the ball in the point zone. The idea is to halt reversal dribbles or passes through the point area by a smothering-type denial defense. With proper and aggressive point coverage, the offense will be forced to use skip passes.

Coaching Tips

1. Folding chairs held by one's wrists behind the neck provide nicely the regimen needed for maintaining hands from reaching. Great drill also for maintaining proper defensive footwork and balance. Instills great confidence in your players' ability to play defense. They reason, "If I can do this with a chair on my back . . ."
2. Constant reminders to your weak-side wings that they should be thinking about and anticipating the steal of the reversal pass or the skip pass, besides dropping back under the basket in help coverage. Most zone offenses are indoctrinated about rapidly moving and swinging the ball. So tell your weak-side wings to have patience and that a little salivating over the upcoming opportunity is normal.
3. In a double high-post offense, practice with your defensive point guard fighting off pins from one or the other posts once the ball is swung.
4. Inside passes against your initial alignment can be devastating. Take measures to instill the importance of keeping arms extended. Your players must understand how important it is to make this entry pass look risky. In practice, have all your players, especially post people, experience the

point position on offense against your extended arms of your 131 zone. Challenge them to attempt to penetrate the zone interior with passes. A picture is worth a . . .

5. A zone defense promotes the taking of offensive charges. Make this a priority of the 131 zone purpose. For every charge my players took in practice and in the games, we recorded them. These became credits for the player. They could barter these credits to be excused from a conditioning drill, they could sell them to other players, and they could carry them forward to the future season. Most are never used for fear that they may need them more later. This became very productive for our team. I wager you will see a few of your players taking charges on players substituting into and out of the game.
6. If the opponent's post has received a pass inside, your defensive rover has the obligation to assist. If the post player puts the ball on the floor, that is a signal for any close players to also assist.
7. Your defense must shift harmoniously; otherwise, gaps and passing lanes appear. This can be somewhat adjusted by coordinating footwork.

A few variations of the 131 Zone

Hard 131. Players #2, 3, and 4 slightly implode their positions. Player #1 plays man-to-man on any offense player with or without the ball in the top zone. The objective is to keep the ball from being rotated, to keep the ball out of the point player's hands, and to encourage long skip passes which are steal-able or allow for time for the defense to adjust rotationally.

Soft 131. Standard formation. Player #1 positions him or herself in the nipple. This ploy is used against high-post danger and/or high-low offenses. The team can compensate by expanding slightly at the wings.

131 Chase. A variation of the 131 Box-and-One. Player position #1 is your designated chaser. Player #4 compensates for this loss of a zone defender by playing his or her position higher than normal. If you need this ploy, the threat is probably not at the high position any longer. Definitely a gimmick defense albeit a sometimes necessary and useful ploy. This defense is useful against a team who initiates most of the plays through one player. Expect the opposition to counter in two ways: First, by implementing a zone offense. Second, by posting up the chased player in a low-post area. Now this area is flooded: two defensive players on one offensive player, leaving someone all alone. It is interesting how this chase defense affects the opposition's hero. Many a "star" explodes under the pressure, and many react to it as something illegal is being done. *The number one goal of the chaser is to deny the hero from the ball.* I remember a league game incident with our rivals at their gym, where a short-tempered opponent, one of those players who could model as a poster child for Planned Parenthood, quit his team during the game. He ran over to his coach, exhausted and complaining over not being able to receive the ball, and then walked off the floor while the game was in play, leaving only four players. We were alternating defensive players each quarter to smother him, denying any easy opportunities for him to receive the ball. Maybe a few sweet nothings of a noncomplimentary nature were whispered in his ear during close contact, but all within legal and ethical limits. He never returned.

131 Flex. Player #2 or #3 play wide enough to force a high lob pass between the offensive point and wing. (See illustration #15.) Player #5, with the aid of the time-consuming lob pass, sprints out to trap the receiver with the assistance of the wing defender. Player #4 quickly slides down the post for frontal coverage on the low-post center that was abandoned by player #5.

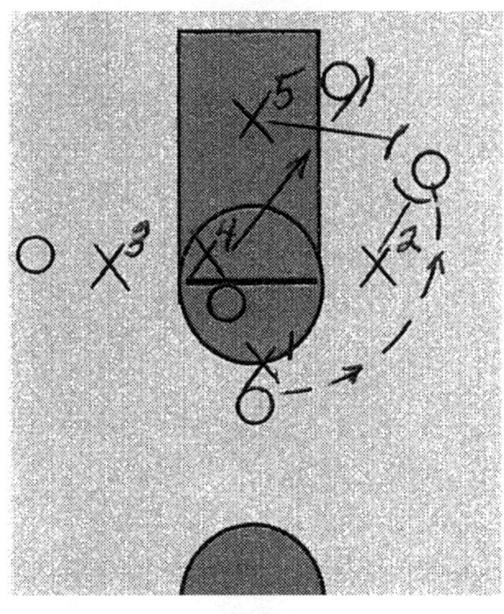

(15)

Player #1 denies the reversal pass to the point. The weak-side wing defender plays the zone area with denial principles. If the trap occurs properly in the corner with two tall defenders, as it should, it is an extremely difficult trap to see over or to pass against.

Jump D is a shift from the 131 zone defense to a smothering man-to-man defense. This shift and change of defensive principles occurs on the first pass to the wing. In the first half of a contest, it may occur arbitrarily when the ball is passed to the left wing, and then in the second half to the opposite side, but only upon the call by your Rover. Most offenses have a difficult time converting from their zone offense to a man-to-man offense from the wing position.

Open Trap (see illustration #16). Upon 10 feet of the offense reaching the midcourt line, player #1 begins forcing the opponent to dribble into a wing-assisted trap. While staying between the opposite offensive guard, he must maintain high hands to discourage this pass. While maintaining this position, wings defenders are instructed to deny the closest receiver one pass away. If their offensive opponent, in their respective zone, is two passes away, then they must collapse to the key area in a help position.

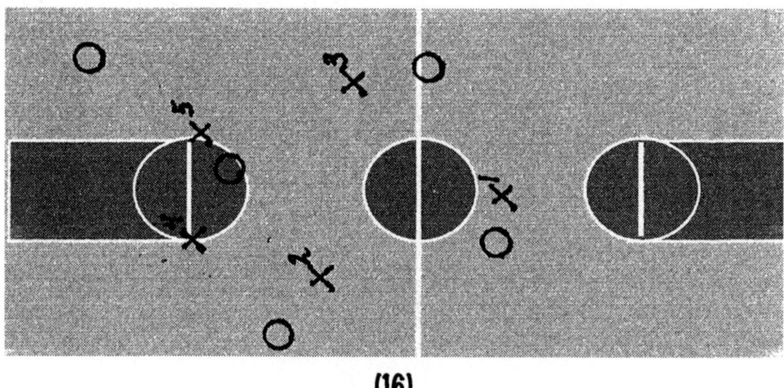

(16)

Let us assume that X1 and X2 trap the offensive guard at the bottom side of the court as shown in illustration #16. Now picture the offensive guard breaking that trap with the dribble. Player X4 would have to break out to reestablish the trap, with player X2 chasing the guard. Now player X5 would have to cover any defender one pass away under or near the basket. Player X1 would be one pass away up high, so he would need to deny any defender in such a position. Player X3 would be two passes away from the penetrating guard, so he would now be playing center field, guarding the basket and playing help defense. And on it would go . . .

Man-To-Man Defense

No matter how good your technique and form, if you are lacking in quick-twitch muscles, everything to do with basketball will be relegated to anticipatory movements. The game is not for the lethargic of mind or energy. It has become a game of quickness and speed. Fortunately for some, quickness can be improved tangibly by drills and intangibly by the proper use and study of anticipation preparation. Speed is apparently God blessed and patented by same.

Many an extremely tall player has failed in reaching the top pinnacles of college ball. Many extremely quick players have risen to the occasion without much height. So if you are planning to use man-to-man defenses with your team, the key to starting is anticipatory lessons. The coaching tactic of watching the dribbler's waist for covering the offensive opponent while on defense is going to accomplish nothing but a good look at the dribbler's caboose as it choo-choos by. Playing the dribbler to his weak side by opening up your stance to influence this move will provide you with an even quicker view of his caboose on the fast track. The offensive player has an advantage over his defender because he knows what he is going to do. The defender has to react, which already puts him in a chase mode. Why would one want to give the dribbler another advantage by opening up one defensive side? You would not; current players can go to their left or right with relative capabilities.

A good stance for man-to-man is in the athlete's position (often described as squatting low enough where someone can barely slide a chair under you). I like a man-to-man stance, which positions the top of your head below the offensive player's chin. Regardless of your quickness, you should play close up against the offensive player who has the ball but has not started the dribble. You should play close enough to not allow a forward step by the dribbler. Man-to-man on the other players is a totally different technique. While up in the ball handler's face, your hands should be responsive to the ball handler's movements. The defender's hand that is on the same side as the ball should be held high on a position over the ball, a stance that would make it difficult to prepare for the shot. The other arm should be bent, with the forearm positioned against the offensive player's waist. The forearm should be used as a steering device as much as your local ordinances allow. It is also for prohibiting the player from swinging the ball from one side to the other. If the player is able to swing the ball to the opposite side of his body, the defender's arms should alternate in compliance, with the opposite hand up and opposite forearm now running the show.

Man-to-man on a pickup play where the dribbler is coming at you at 19 miles per hour has to be played differently lest you pick up a cold from the breeze created as he shoots by you. As I mentioned in the chapter "Practice Tips" under the "Chair Drill," you need to position yourself in front of the ball. You must also be in a full retreat motion before picking up the dribbler. Full retreat is a seemingly difficult idea for players. Most defenders would rather try to play "Mexican Ole," a defensive bullfighting stance without footwork that requires reaching out with one hand in an attempt to steal the ball. Then as the player continues by, you yell "Ole!" Keep your defensive player in front of the ball, defending the dribble, not the player. This will tie up the offensive ball handler with crossover dribbles, slowing him down and making the ball vulnerable to the steal. Once you start fronting the offensive man, the ball is now past you and you are chasing instead of defending.

Man-to-man on offensive players without the ball is coached in many ways depending on the aggressiveness of the coach's style. A one-pass-away defensive ploy may be a mugging-style stance, one that the defender uses his bent arm on the back side of the offensive player to inhibit an offensive backdoor cut. His arm toward the passer is extended with the thumb pointed downward, in front of the man he is guarding, for stealing or slapping the potential incoming pass and for a little further control of the receiver.

A less aggressive man-to-man on a player without the ball is called using "pistols." You collapse off your defender and position your body so that one hand can be pointed at the ball and the other at the man you are covering. This forms a triangle between you, your man, and the ball. The angles become less acute and more obtuse the further you become from the ball. The premise to this gunslinger position is that it places you in proper position for guarding your man and helping your teammates. Because of federal gun laws, you probably cannot cross the border with this defense? This is not a functional position for post defense, for it allows offensive players to flash in front of their defender. It is better for post people, when helping, to position themselves on a straight line between their offensive man and the ball. Coaching your post defender to play like his head was on a swivel is important. This eliminates the surprises of back flashes from occurring while in this position.

Some coaches prefer for their defensive post man to defend the offensive post man by playing behind him. This deters an alley-oop pass, which—when received—leaves no inside coverage on the post man. Some coaches prefer their defensive post man to play in front of the offensive post man to stop the entry pass and force the alley-oop pass. Other coaches prefer a three-quarter coverage much like the defense employed at the wing position. My decision on which style to use depended on my talent. If we had a very tall post player, we would allow the entry pass for obvious reasons. If my help defender was capable, we would front or sandwich the post man who was looking for the entry pass. If my post defender was in foul trouble, we would front or three-quarter the offensive post.

Man-to-man defense is sometimes employed to stop the opponent from fast-breaking. To do so, each player guards the opponent that is guarding him. That allows immediate coverage after a shot, for you spend no time looking for your man to defend on the break because he has been beside you, guarding you on defense. This is good rational for-fast breaking against teams that want to play half-court zone. Their defenders will not be harassing your inlet and/or outlet passes. They will be concerned with sprinting downcourt to their zone positions. Look for players with their backs to you. They generally continue that pose as the game goes on. This is something that you can talk to your team about and take advantage of eventually. Contrary to what many think, man-to-man defense slows the tempo of a full-court game. It does not encourage the pass as full-court zone defenses do. Much more dribbling occurs than passing. Which is the quicker transportation method?

Chapter 6

Offensive Quick Hitters and Shooting Tips

Unlike football where you personally call every play right down to controlling the first step of every player and controlling when he makes that step and controlling the angle and direction of each player's movement, in a basketball game, you sit back, watch, and supervise. The preparation in practices is where you do your coaching. Basketball is an action-reaction contest that is best played without your constant intervention, which—in reality—is always too late; it is played best without it. Basketball players play best when they are merely acting and reacting to situations and not looking over their shoulders for their coach's instructions. The contests are too fast; basketball players do not have the luxury of twenty-five-second breaks between each basket attempt to discuss the next tactic. (Your rewards for successful shots are two points from the field and one point from the free-throw line and have been since 1895-96. The NCAA saw it in its wisdom, in 1979-80, to add one point to the two-point shot when made from 19 feet and 9 inches, or *further.)* Basketball is a novel sport to coach.

Basketball coaches lack the control that other type coaches enjoy such as in tennis, baseball, and golf. Basketball coaching is best done between games. You coach your players at practices and try to assimilate every situation that might occur. Once the game starts, you let them have the reins. You have to let them go solo and hope your practice lessons were properly planned, presented correctly, and received well. Once the game clock begins, you become a supervisor, one who strives to keep control and to keep their players within the game plan. However, once the fledgling has been nudged over the edge of the nest by its mother, the training is over.

Advise your young players to let the game come to them. Take advantage of situations, but don't force them; let the situations occur and come to, then react accordingly within the team game plan. "Shake and bake" moves within the team concept occur on fast breaks. In the half-court game, excessive shake-and-bake moves are discouraged; the only thing cooking will be turnovers and not of the pastry type. An independent read or personal ad-lib out of the offense is normally looked on in favor by the coaching staff as long as it comes out of normal options previously discussed.

On an independent shake-and-bake move, one that is not part of the offense, your teammates are going to be confused. If they don't know what you are doing, the rebound spots are probably not being filled properly. Again, you are back in the kitchen; now the only thing cooking is hot dogs. Granted, no coach wants his players to play so robotically that imaginative options are missed. As a coach, you need to monitor, early and closely, the quantity and quality of freedom displayed by your players; otherwise, your trainer's kit is going to overflow with mustard and catsup instead of pre-wrap and tape.

If a shake-and-bake move is executed, it should be done properly. One quick fake and a hard ballistic move to the basket. This type of move catches every one off guard. To use too many fake moves, especially those that involve defensive dribbling *(dribbling without advancing, commonly seen occurring back and forth between one's legs)* only summons weak side defensive help to snuff your eventual move. I enjoy coaching up-tempo basketball. Because of that fact and because believe that if you are shooting the ball, you are not throwing it away. A fast-breaking, pressing program, win or lose (a few), is loved by the most fickle fans. During pursuit of a loose ball and you see nothing but $%#holes and elbows of your players in chase of it brings a swelling of pride in coaches. When you first view your newborn, assuming you're married, you will not jump up and begin clapping like you do for the extreme efforts of capturing a loose ball.

Most of my favorite man-to-man offensive plays are quick hitters. They are especially productive when used after a motion or a controlled option play. I have two favorite man-to-man offenses to share. I have one quick-hitting zone offense to add. The first offense is called "Down." It is a man-to-man offense run out of the standard double low post. Because of the feature of your quicker players lined up low, this play can be run out of your early offense or as a situation play. (See illustration #17)

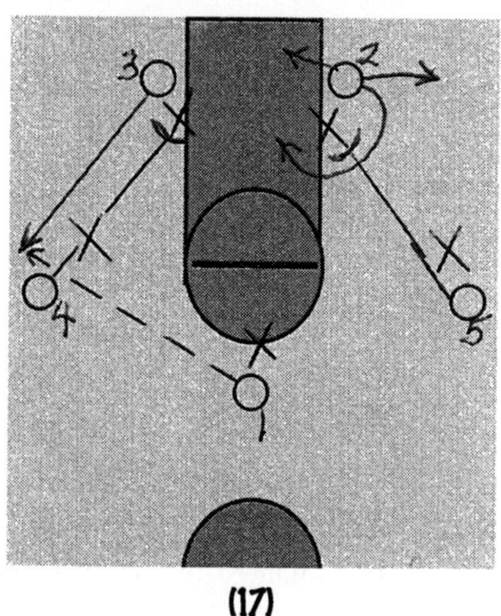

(17)

Roles

Every player should be cognizant of floor space. Keep the defense spread. All the players in this offense should be shooters or at least scorers.

O1 is your point guard who has much authority because of his position and sight advantage over the play options we use. He should be quick and intelligent. At halftime of games, he will be quizzed over mismatches he has noted and expected to be able to discuss in length those plays that were most favorable for the team offense.

O4 and O5 are your post players. They should be your tallest floor players. Naturally, they should be good rebounders. They need to be accomplished backboard shooters. These two players must be able to play with their backs to the basket. They should be well-trained in catching high passes using the 'block and snatch' method discussed in the chapter "Practice Tips." They need to be good passers off the screen (pick-and-roll).

O2 and O3 are your best outside shooters. They should also be adept at driving. These players should be tall and quick. They should be adept at "read-bounding" on the move. It is important that they read well off of down screens. They will be called on for deciding whether to cut, curl, or flare off those screens. This will be explained in detail under rotations.

Rules

The offense is called off whenever our point has a position advantage on his defender. He drives, everyone spreads; if he dishes or kicks out, everyone sprints to rebound the shot.

Rotations

The play begins with **O4 and O5** down screening for **O2 and O3.** It is important that **O2 and O3** hold their positions long so that the screen exchanges are as low down the free-throw line as possible and still outside the three-second count. Once **O4 and O5** have set their screens, they need to pivot and pin the defenders. These screeners do not merely trade places with the teammates they are screening for; they are heat-seeking missiles locked in on opponents—they are "cruisin' to a bruisin'." The down screeners make good physical contact (we call these screens "bangs" to get across to our players that they must be physical on these encounters to contain and hold the defenders). We coach the screeners to use crossed arms for "banging," and then they pivot and extend those crossed arms to control the defender with their backside, an aggressive controlling hold with the backside of the arms, a move that even a competent referee would not whistle on you. The screener's goal is twofold: one to pin the opponent and furthermore to free their teammate.

O2 and O3 will have the first reads off these initial screens. As their teammates come down to set their "bangs," they reach out to grab that teammate by the waist. They use their inside arm for grasping and then continue holding as they come off the screen. They have three options depending on their defender's reaction. First, if the defender follows him, then he continues to hold his teammate and swings around him with the help of the hold and curls to the basket, looking for a pass from the point guard. Furthermore, if the defender cheats and slides off the screen to the inside, then O2 or O3 flares out toward the corner to await the point guard's pass for a short jumper. Moreover, if the defender fights through the inside or anticipates the screen movement, then O2 or O3 reverses flight and fakes the screen and cuts back to the basket with arm held high as a target. On your flare or cut move, the point guard has the option of hitting O4 or O5 if they are holding good pins for a good post-up play. It has to be a good pin. The pass will be chancy without the post coming to the ball. In that case, either O2 or O3 will need to clear out. Prepare for the "read-bound," for as you know, once a post man gets the ball inside, it's like trying to get something out of a Stephen Hawking black hole. If nothing develops from the cut, curl, and flare and the post receives nothing, then the wing comes out high to O4's or O5's original positions and we run a pick-and-roll between the post and wing. The scramble offense can easily be incorporated into this offense if you wish more continuation with more screens. Another quick-hitting offense is the *one-four set.* This offense is designed to spread the floor for a backdoor look or double-post play. Even though the double-post play is a valuable part of this offense, this is mainly an offense for a team short on height.

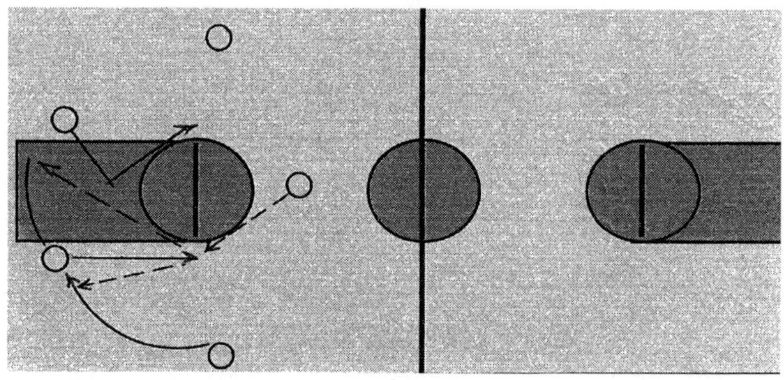

(18)

Roles

This offense is designed for quick one-on-one openings. (See illustration 18.) It is imperative that your wings are well spread. They should be two or three feet from the sidelines. They should also be back from the free-throw line, extended at least ten feet or more depending on their speed. The necessity of the widespread look is not so much for isolating offensive players with defensive players, albeit important, but for using space for additional speed. Another reason for the exaggerated spread—especially with high school players—is that they tend to cheat and narrow the floor to be closer to the action, or they just get lazy.

Rules

If our point guard is being overplayed much like in our play "Down," he attacks the basket, expecting a dish situation or a three-on-three look. Unlike "Down," we don't expect to "kick out" with this set because our personnel are so far extended. If we can get a three-on-three situation around the basket, there would be no need for improving this advantage.

Rotations

Once the play has been initiated by both posts flashing to the free-throw elbows, the point guard has a read option. If both posts are covered, and well they may be, they probably have lob pass options. If covered, which seldom occurs because the defender is worried about the lob pass, a simple quick reversing of post positions will provide a pin, enabling the point with a safe pass. However, you would prefer this not to happen. For the backdoor play to work, it is important that your misdirection of movement is still occurring as the post pass is received. Give your post people various methods of getting to the elbows unescorted for the safe quick pass. The pass into the post should be off of a look toward the wing; once that is sold, a no-look flip into the approaching post will best deliver the backdoor option. Immediately after the look by the point guard and the gesture of selling a receiving posture by the wing, that wing needs to make a ballistic swim move on his defender and attack the basket. The post man then bounce passes the ball to the wing in plenty of time and distance from the basket. The wing's fast approach makes necessary an early pass. A right-handed wing needs to time his catch so that his body is in the air with his right foot forward. This is called the "pop step move." Once the ball hits him, he can glide, land, and take another full step to enter his shot motion. He can protect the ball with both hands and begin focusing on his target early in his approach. This all can happen from fifteen feet or further without the use of a dribble, depending on the speed and athleticism of your wing. If the wing is covered, the play is still available. An accurate bounce pass directly at the lead foot of the wing's defender is impossible to intercept because when one is running at that speed, he is negated the ability to bend over far enough to intercept the pass. The ball will bounce upward to the covered wing for a playable catch. If the pass is uncertain by the post man, then he must wait. My experience is that once the wing passes under the basket, the defender's intensity wanes. The defender knows this play from childhood, seeing it on the playgrounds many times. By the time the wing nears the basket, the defender knows it is too late for the pass and slows down. This constant need for the conservation of motion that players feel they need to store creates the demise of many a defender. This is always a mistake and a great second look for the offense. The post man needs to reverse pivot and look for his wing coming out from under the other side of the basket. The post usually has an easy bounce pass to the now-open wing.

Back to the entry pass to the post from the point. Immediately on that catch, the opposite post needs to cut to the basket. It has to happen quickly because of the speed of the attacking wing who assuredly wants the ball. With some teams, we found this short pass to be highly successful, more so than the backdoor pass that it was set up to exploit. With other teams, this short post-to-post never turned up; I guess it just depends on your personnel. If the post is being overcovered for the entry pass, lob it over him, for there can be no one behind him. Oh yeah, easy two points. Our zone offense, which we called "Spartan" (I don't remember where the name got its derivation), was simple but effective. Because of its ability to present three-point shots and easy close looks, we seldom saw teams stay in zones against us. (See illustration #19.)

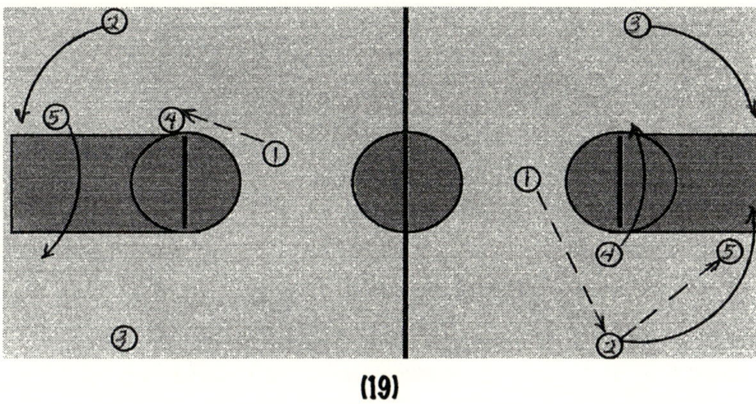

(19)

It was up to everyone to work together on running this zone offense as high as possible. Each time the defense accommodated us, we would try to extend it even higher.

Roles

O1 made certain that the ball was reversed often and quick. We did not want the defense to rest from its necessary matchups. The quicker the point-to-wing reversal pass, the more often the wing was placed in a one-on-one situation. It was up to O1 to take advantage of the zone shifting for direct entry passes to our posts coming off of their pins. O1 also made sure that the zone could not pack in by being prepared and eager to shoot. O1's ball movement was designed to be positioned over the gaps of the zone for initiating plays. We discouraged our point of returning a wing pass to the same wing; this allowed the defense from having to move, even but for a second.

O2 and O3: Most of our drives against zone defenses occurred from the wings. The quick skip pass from wing to wing could provide one-on-one situations. Once the skip reached the wing, it was difficult for the zone to recover over that distance. Our wings were coached to backdoor attack once our entry passes reached the post men. When our wings were in control of the ball, they had four passing options. They could reverse the ball through the point. They could skip pass to the opposite side. They could drive down to the baseline, staying far from the key. We called that move "testing the waters." It tended to flatten out the zone, giving the wing different passing looks; and lastly, they had entry pass options to our post men off their pins. Of course, they were free to shoot when given good looks by the defense when our rebounders were in reasonable positions.

O4 was the better of our passing posts. His main role was to pick up pins against defensive guards. For example, against a 2-3 or 2-1-2 zone, if he was posted at an elbow of the key and the ball was reversed to a weak side wing, his first responsibility was to pivot and pin the opposite defensive guard. He would then be open for an easy entry pass. He becomes a very dangerous player with the ball in that location. He needed to possess an accurate short jump shot. If our low post received a pass, O4 would fight to slide across the key under the guards.

O5 was our tallest player and best scorer from under the basket. If O4 received a pass, O5 would scrape across the key, fighting over the low-post defenders. At the same time, our strong-side wing would fill the emptied post position like a backdoor cut.

Rules

As mentioned earlier, we discouraged return passes to the wings from our point. These passes caused practically no defensive or adjusting motion from the zone. If the left wing threw a pass directly to the point, nothing was accomplished by passing the ball back to the same wing. The defense did not have to move from their positions. In addition, it slowed down our perimeter movement, which is necessary for providing entry looks. Our perimeter people were coached not to try an entry pass until the ball had been reversed a few times. Passing lanes become visible from defenses that tire, and gaps become visible from defenses with unequal personnel quickness. Our wings were instructed to play at different depths, which included "testing the waters" to create different passing looks. Anytime a post person received an entry pass, he was to pivot and square to the basket—a necessity.

Rotations

Once the pass went to a wing, the respective zone defenders three- quartered our posts or totally fronted them. Once the ball was reversed, we coached our posts to momentarily hold their positions with opponents now on their backs. Now they are positioned for a simple entry pass, but it must be made quickly before the defender recovers. Again, any time a post person received a pass, the opposite post flashed across the key. Again, when a ball went to the low post, the high post would flash across by sliding under the defense. If the high post received the ball, the low post would flash across the key by scraping over the low defender. Anytime the posts received the ball, our wings crashed, simulating a backdoor movement. Once the ball was reversed, our posts flashed to the strong side. Sometimes, they flashed straight across; other times, diagonally. It depended on the situations. Against some teams, we wanted our low post to stay low; against others, it didn't matter. There was no advantage on getting open by staggering the flashing manners; but occasionally, against certain teams, it did create matchup problems. An interesting zone offense you may like to study or implement into your offense is the "over-load-box." It provides a plethora of shooting opportunities from outside, from post ups and cutting looks. I have seen many teams, out of frustration, leave their zone defenses to man up for better defending this offense. There is not much motion involved with this offensive set, except for player O1 who is very mobile.

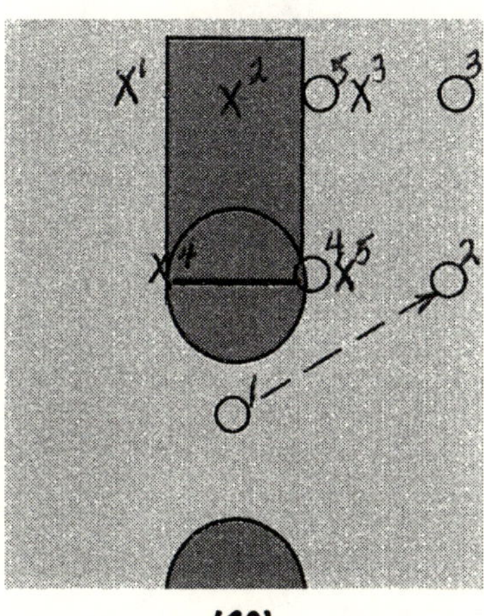

(20)

O4 and O5 should be very imaginative players regarding picking up post pins. O1 needs to be coached at hitting post people with passes from the weak side after receiving long skip passes to the weak side. O1 also flirts with penetration into the paint without the ball. (See illustration #20.) Imagine that your team is in a two-three zone, as shown above. Develop the rotations necessary for covering the above offensive positions with your players. Before you do, note that O3 and O2 can bury the ball at will. Don't cheat on them, for they can fill it up. Recognize that O1 plays very mobile between the point and all spots in the key, including under the basket. What problems did you come across? Have you found that it is difficult for X1 to cover O1 from shots in the paint? Imagine further how your team would adjust while under game pressure without your advice or time-out. We always experimented with this offense against zones early in the game to see if we were going to get three-point looks and to see how they covered our point. As many times as we saw teams jump to man-to-man, it still surprised me.

Offensive Coaching Tips

1. Coach your low-post players to raise a hand when they are coming out to set a back screen. For a split second, the defender of that post man is duped into believing that the post man is asking for a pass. This delays the warning from the defender to his teammate about the screen. Just before the contact of the screen, have your post screener reach out and tap the opposite side of the person being screened (a Globetrotter staple that always works against the Washington Generals). This may create another split second of confusion to the opponents. To add to the confusion, you can have your screener pull an Alex Rodriguez vocal sham, "I've got it!" Only in basketball nomenclature, it would sound like "Pick right, pick right!" when in fact, you are setting a screen left. Why not? This is not character-rich golf we are playing.
2. When coming off a back screen, coach your players to make good shoulder contact with each other so they don't allow the defender to fight through the screen. Much like the contact of your driving point guard on his defender, where he lowers and brushes his shoulder against the opponent's hip.
3. Anytime you are running a backdoor from the point position to your wing, look directly at your receiver first and try to sell a pass to that player. Have that player react with a pass receiving gesture, hands out, to further sell the false play. In reaction to the fake, the wing's defender will overplay him to deny the pass. This overplay will make it much easier for your backdoor receiver to get open for a direct or indirect pass. Without the

aforementioned acting, it is possible for the wing to isolate himself with a simple, good physical swim-over move. On the right side of the court, this would require the offensive player to reach out to the defender's waist with his left hand, immobilizing him, and then swinging the right hand over the opponent's head—works every time. Another slower opening move works by the offensive player taking a long step between the defender's legs, close to his groin, and then reverse pivoting to situate your back to his waist to find yourself enjoying an advantageous pin. Then with a slight bump or nudge with your rump, you should be on your way to the basket without a tail. You may want to look at the clock first and ascertain there is plenty of time for this operatic move.

4. Always coach your guards to bring the ball downcourt fast. Seldom do beneficial mistakes happen without pressure on the defense. Quite often, with an attacking guard, a post defender will pop out to help, leaving his man open under the basket without weak-side defensive help. You never know?
5. Always assign two people responsible for defending the cherry pickoff of botched plays. Your point guard should have a genetic instinct for this role. However, when he is attacking and kicking out, no matter what his DNA sample provides, he is going to need help for covering the opponent's streaker (*no pun intended)* Your wing people must go from auxiliary point work to regular-duty point work. This is a difficult area to coach; once you learn your personnel, set some definite antiharvesting roles.
6. Don't fear leaving your offense. Be malleable offensively. More important, be willing to change on little notice, and be willing to accept error for this change. For example, a very short player should be exploited on defense. Post this player up, and see how well he can defend under the basket. Because this short person's mother is in the crowd should not temper your ferociousness on attacking the hobbit. Part of being a successful coach is harboring a little ruthlessness for exploiting advantages. Turnaround is more than fair game. I believe that it is necessary for a team to accept an opponent's success. Those times that we were not handling another team's press very well, if the game was lost, I would speak to the opposing coach to continue their press, regardless of the score. I would explain to our players that we obviously needed more of this full-court press exposure so no team in the future could catch us unprepared for this press scheme. There are many offensive systems to adapt to your personnel. You must first

learn about your player's strengths and weaknesses. *The most dangerous offensive position in basketball is the high post.* When the ball is in the hands of the high-post man, in the high center of the key area, many difficult denial defensive positions are presented. Flashes are extremely difficult to cover. Every defender must play deny defense and is drawn from helping. An offensive zone ploy used by the single high-post offense is offensive pins by the post man. Difficult to defend if the post man pins correctly. Against even zones (221 or 23), the high post will command attention from the high guard on the strong side; then when the ball is reversed, the post will find the weak-side guard on his back whom he will retain there, providing him a very advantageous position for a pass. When the high post has the ball, it truly creates many different and difficult stances needed for deny defense. If that is true, you might want to give a look at your personnel regarding adopting the high-post offense or adapting its principles to your offense. It worked well for a Wizard in Westwood.

Offensive Shooting

Coach your players to develop high-percentage backboard shots. Design your plays to position your players for these shots when and wherever possible. Backboard shots at 50-degree angles or under are, at reasonable distances, more accurate shots than swish attempts at the basket. *(The 6 × 4 foot backboard was approved in the rules of 1906-07; earlier backboards were introduced in 1893.)*

Three axioms for the backboard shot:

1. Unlike your defender, with a backboard shot, you know where the rebound is going to come off. The higher percentage of these missed shots come off the front of the basket. A good defender, on release of the ball, will screen out between you and the basket. The backboard shot nullifies the screener's action because the backboard shooter does not follow his shot on a line. He scampers at an angle off the defender's screen to the front of the basket. This nullifies the defenders straight on to the basket screen-out position.
2. A shot aimed at the middle of the basket is a depth-perception guess. Depth perception is not as an affecting decision on the backboard shot. You

have a spot to aim at on the backboard, which does not call on perception guessing. On a basket attempt, an overshot is likely to miss as is a short soft shot. With the backboard shot, a missed overshot still has a chance of success, while a high short shot also has a chance. Sight perception is greatly reduced, which is an advantage for less accurate shooters.

3. Hardness of shot is no longer the consideration that it is for a net shot. Good type of shot for a player just entering the game or for a nervous shooter.

Backboard Shot Drill

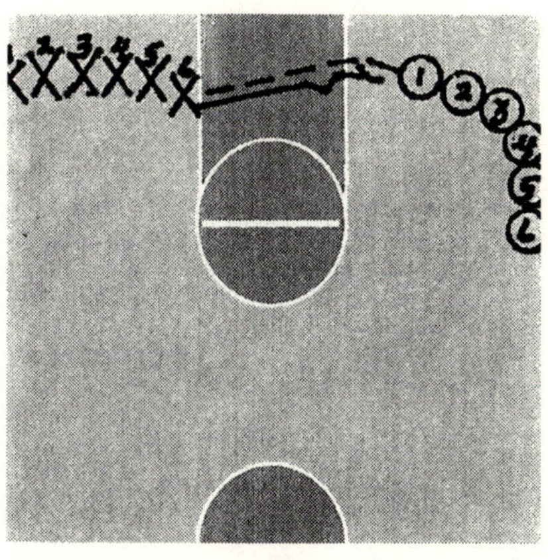

(21)

X6 passes to O1 and sprints to defend O1's backboard shot. After O1 shoots, both players fight for the rebound and put back. Only one put back shot. (See illustration #21.) The defender X6 recovers the made or missed shot and outlets to O1 who has already popped out to the sideline as high as the free-throw line extended. O1 has already commanded for the ball with a loud "Outlet!" If O1 missed his shot, both players run the floor. If he made his shot, both players are excused from running the floor, and they return to the end of the opposite lines. X1 now skip passes the ball to O2 after the loud command "Ball!" by O2. O2 dribble advances to the block and then, with a jump, stop puts up the backboard jump shot. During the skip pass, X5 attacks the shooter, finishing in a good close out stance. And so it goes on, The jump shot, when properly executed, is very difficult to defend. However, before coaching the jump shot, it is important to master the jump stop. This balanced stop is one of the most important moves to develop for a basketball player. The jump stop is a prerequisite for the running jump shot. We all know what the jump stop is, but very few can execute it well on the run. The jump stop takes much practice.

Coming to a stop without establishing a pivot foot and maintaining your balance is difficult for even the most seasoned gym rat. It takes a leap in the air to convert the motion to a controlled stop, much like the gather step just before a lay in. It requires landing on the heels, which is unique, and then rolling forward to the balls of the feet. A rocking forward motion that is performed in a crouched position. No pivot foot is established with the jump stop, thus you are not limited from a crossover move or pivot move if you are stopped from shooting. A very difficult shot to defend. The jump stop should be executed with a thrusting up of the ball to a shooting position. This quick movement throws off the balance of the defender, fearing the shot is about to occur. If you are pivoting or crossing out of this position, the shot thrust will draw your opponent out of his crouched stance to a less functional extended stance. It is now easier to take advantage of the defense with a pivot or crossover. The reverse pivot is led with the snapping of the head to increase focus time for the shot or pass.

Once a player has mastered the jump stop, he can work on *the simplest but most difficult shot in basketball to defend. It is the speed dribble jump-stop shot.* As a defender, when the ball is dribbled full speed straight at you and that player abruptly stops with a jump stop, how do you defend it? You cannot anticipate that shot, because the attacking nature of the drive has you concerned about first stopping the drive. Then the jump-stop shooter elevates straight up with arms high in his execution. Again, what can you do? Pete Maravich was an exemplary possessor of this shot, and we know the success he reaped from this move. The Pistol played before tattoos were required for entering the NBA. If the move comes off a good jump stop, taking a charge is eliminated.

Another difficult move to stop is the jump-stop crossover step and the jump-stop reverse-pivot step. Both of these moves include bringing the ball high in a shooting position. Again, in both of these situations, you are attacking the defense. If the defender is on his heels, you are open for using the jump-stop crossover step to pass by the opponent. If the defender attacks you or crowds you on the jump-stop, the reverse-pivot will be necessary for spinning by the opponent. This move is somewhat embarrassing to the opponent. An "excuse me" or a "pardon me" is probably appropriate during this demeaning move.

Alternate shooting drills are to be at the beginning of practice when your players are fresh and at the end of practice when your players are tired. Watch what they learn. When fresh, your shooting target is the middle of the basket. When tired, we recommend shooting at the backside of the basket and using more leg force.

Beside adapting an offense to your personnel, you need an offense that complements or suits your defense. If you are set on double teaming and trapping presses, you probably need to look at quick scoring offenses. You want a juggernaut offense that is capable of scoring off of turnovers at a fast pace. You also need an offense that keeps up the tempo of your defense. Vice versa with a nonattacking defense. If your defensive scheme employs little gambling, your offensive counter should be a controlled pass pattern or a multiscreen patterned design. Each possession becomes more important than the attacking sort, thus this offense demands a controlled attack, which demands good looks for high-percentage shots.

Chapter 7

Slow Hitters

"Doubles Left and Right" is a simple offense for expanding a lead or for using against a man-to-man defense that inclines to spread and deny or for controlling the tempo of a game (accelerating the game or for sitting on the ball.) It has advantages that a short team can use over a tall defensive team. It is not necessarily designed for short teams. Both tall and short teams can take advantage of the opportunities that this offense offers. It provides many backdoor plays and three-point opportunities. A versatile point guard will be given many looks for exploiting various one-on-one situations. A necessary element of this offense is a talented point guard. Without this type of player, I would not recommend this offense. This offense can take control of the game, especially if you are sitting on a three—or four-point lead. (See illustration #22.)

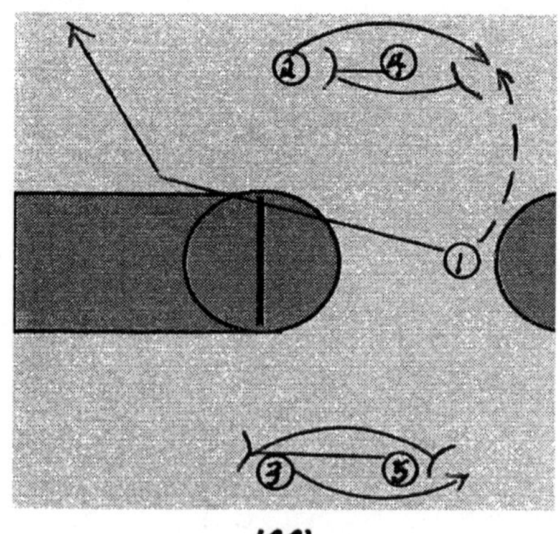

(22)

Roles

O1 has to be the near consummate point guard type. He should be strong off the dribble, with excellent one-on-one qualities, and a good closer. O2 and O3 should have good driving and passing qualities. Both should be adept at three-point shooting. O4 and O5 should be strong screeners and capable of closing after rolling off screens.

Rules

O3 and O2 need to spread the floor. They need to set up a minimum 22 feet from the baseline and 6 feet from the sideline. They should mimic this spread each time down the floor and not have to be reminded of it by the coaches. Their use of the floor determines the success of this offense. O4 and O5 set up even higher. They also need to be six feet from the sideline, but another 3 or 4 feet higher than their teammates O2 and O3. O1 needs to attack down the floor every possession, not too far past the midcourt line unless, of course, he has beaten his defender on a drive to the basket. This aggressive move is important for your teammate's options as later explained under rotations. Once this very structured offense is established, everyone must stay to their assigned roles except for O1.

Rotations

The offense begins after the point guard has tested the openness of the defense and has decided not to challenge it further. O4 and O5 simultaneously break down to set down screens on the defenders of O2 and O3. Both O2 and O3 break outside of their screens to receive the pass from O1. Just as O2 or O3 receives the pass, still approximately six or seven feet from the sideline, their teammates O4 and O5 release their prior screens; they pivot and come out higher to again screen for O2 or O3 to attack the basket on a classic-style pick-and-roll move.

After O1 passes to either O2 or O3, he cuts down through to the basket, asking for the ball. If he does not receive the return pass, he continues to the corner of the same side of the floor to which he just passed. He sets up there to await a pass for the three-point attempt.

If the ball at this point is in the hands of O2 and he elects not to attack the basket with O5, then he hits O3 who has timed it to come off his last screen from O4 and crosses the court for the pass from O2 at O1's original and now-vacant position. O1 leaves the corner to come out to O2's original position. Now the play is reset with O3 at the point, and all options are renewed.

Coaching Tips

The independent play of the point guards, except for your top guard, should be somewhat discouraged once the defense is reset and under control. Of course this depends on your confidence in those handling the ball. The longer this offense runs, the more options will present themselves. Defenses seem to lose intensity on their coverages. Defenses also become accustomed to the motion and tend to cheat for attempting steals, oblivious to the options they will meet. I said earlier that this offense can also accelerate a team's lead. This is true; however, the nature of its options, to accelerate or stall, presents some coaching difficulties. It is difficult to show the options for scoring and then expect your players to forego them when stalling. Good luck. However, once mastered by your players, it is a do-all offense against man-to-man defenses. We called this play "Smart"—I guess as a subliminal message for reminding the players of the purpose of this offense.

There will be times when your team just cannot make shots. Normally, these occurrences happen only during important games. Be prepared for these days and hope that your opponents are coached by a dyed-in-the-wool man-to-man coach. Your team's preparation for those nightmarish occurrences should be a conversion for playing a low-post offensive game or a slow-down game. That means that your team is going to obligingly give up the outside shots. I have always reminded my players that they cannot expect to be efficient in shooting every contest. However, they can always rely on defense. Defense is not judged on percents, nor does it rely on fine touch. It is a tough part of the game that is hard to summon; however, it is not a fine part of the game whereby after the game, one questions where his defense went. If you play hard, you can always count on your defense to be there. I remember, at a first game of the state tournament where one of my teams fell into that wasteland of shooting, where we could not find an offense to reward us; fortunately, the other team was just as cold. At the end of the first quarter, neither team had over five or six points. The only good balls hit were by a rake that I had stepped on earlier that morning. At the first-quarter break, we discussed nothing but defense with the team. We felt that if we could continue this defense, we had the game under wraps. Nothing was said about shooting, just about picking up the "D." Both teams went on with their dismal shooting for the remainder of the game, but we focused our frustrations on playing wild and aggressive physical defense, and it worked.

Chapter 8

Tactics

Tactics are a constant challenge to the basketball coach. They are always changing, seldom new, but a subject for your attention. The only thing you can count on in life is change. Nothing changes as much as American technology or American basketball. Technology change is an exponential result motivated by money. Basketball change occurs because people just can't leave a good thing alone. For some reason, the "powers that be" cannot keep their hands off basketball. Even though it is a great draw, basketball people seems to believe annual facelifts will keep the game young, all designed to make the game faster. I'm glad they have had no influence with the game Monopoly. I can't imagine Monopoly played with the pressure of a dice clock. They don't mess with the "American pastime." Granted, there have been a few changes: mitts are a little larger, and steroids have replaced salt pills. A Yankee-Red Sox game will flirt with three hours of game time, not counting batting cage time. Football has not changed radically since Gus Dorais found Knute Rockne on a ten-yard bomb against Army, back when pigs shied from stadiums to keep their bladders. Buy a national basketball rules book and look at the first fifty pages: all points of interest for new changes. Each year, this enigma continues.

I come from the snapping twine era. Do you remember, on a "swish shot," when the nets would hang up on the rim, slowing down the fast break? Now they have nonwhip nets to speed up the action. Jocks and Socks have been replaced by thigh-high clinging undergarments. The "key" is large enough for passing lanes, and a favorite basketball game called Bump has been changed to Ultimate Bump, which allows players knocked out to reenter if the player that knocked them out gets knocked out—whew. Basketball players now pump iron or try to act like it. Two speed-up facets of the game are the increased number of teams using full-court pressure and fast-breaking.

One thing that has never changed for the hoop junkie, thanks be, are the sounds from a basketball gym. The unmistakable sounds of basketball shoes squeaking against multivarnished hardwood floors. When you blend those sounds with the gymnasium echoes of a bouncing basketball from those hardwood floors and then add a few swishes of snapping twine from made shots, you know you are close to heaven. Why have they not made a background song from those sounds? I'd buy it!

Another contributor to the acceleration of the game is the full-court press. This penchant for stalking players the full 90 feet of the court can be very hazardous for the unprepared offense. For the prepared, it is but a slight nuisance. For illustrative preparatory means, imagine, on a court the size of a football field, how difficult it would be to press or beat a press. Obviously, no zone presses would be effective. There could be no weak-side helping, and there could be no double-teaming, for that would mean leaving players in wide open spaces without a defender. The defense would be relegated to man -to-man pressing only. If your offense could not beat these presses, you have more problems than the press to deal with. On a court the size of a house, any type press would be difficult to navigate. Agree? With ten ball players in a tight, enclosed space, there would be few passing lanes that couldn't close immediately. Getting to open spaces would be more difficult than getting to a cash register at Macy's on Christmas eve. Agree? Then design your press break that spreads all ten players across the full court. Do not, even for a short time, compress all your players into the half court. There are situations where you might, as a ruse, like the one-four alignment where two players sprint to the other end. Cute plays like these normally accomplish little, except for putting the seed of thought into the fans and athletic director that you are going wacko. Ideally, a two-on-two situation in the backcourt would be most pragmatic and advantageous for the offense. A one-on-one is not going to occur, for there are no trapping scenarios for this much space with only two players, so the defense would not accommodate you.

So with the aid of basic math ratios, to optimize working space, you will need to send two men deep to attract a like number of defenders. The defense is now spread and is forced to provide you possible passing lanes without bringing an extra player down from backcourt. This would open up too much space in the backcourt. Stay away from a press break that accumulates ten men, not counting the referees, in the half court. Your only break will be heartbreak, watching your players stumble, fumble, and turn over passes.

Two-zone press breaks that have been successful by our teams:

1. Against a 131 or diamond press, your guards need to play catch (keep away) against the point defender all the way up the court, looking to create a gap. With each guard-to-guard pass, the passer needs to step back as a release receiver for the other guard and as a defender in case of a turnover by your teammate. Once the gap is enlarged, a dribble attack will open this defense, creating passing weaknesses.
2. Versus even presses, two front defenses, such as the 221 and 212, we set up in a matching set. Two offensive players would set up in the backcourt spread wide and two in the front court, spread wide.

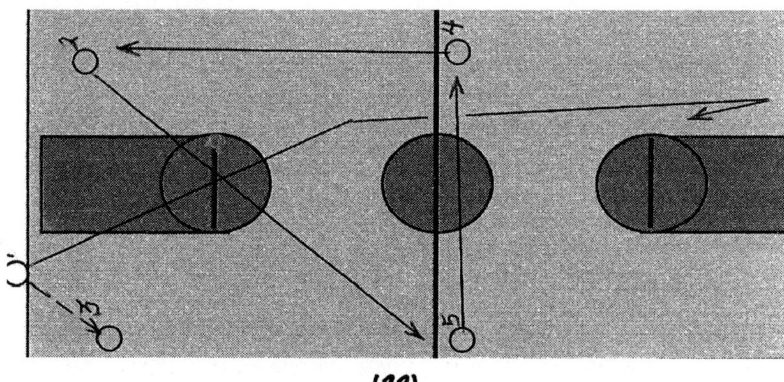

(23)

Our entry pass would be to O2 or O3. (See illustration #23.) They could screen switch off of each other to get open. At that point, we ran a continuous rotation break. The direction depended on which guard received the entry pass. Let's imagine that O3 received the entry pass. O2 would then flash diagonally to O5's location. O4 would break to the end line to O2's empty location. O5 would sprint to O4's now-vacant position. O1 would follow O2 from a distance, approximately 7 or 8 feet behind O2. Once to the midcourt line, O1 would clear out to the opposite end of the court. O3, who has the ball, is looking to pass to either middle cutters O2 or O1. He also has a skip pass option to O5.

If none of the cutters are open, the opposite guard position will become open; in this example, it will be O4. After the pass to O4, O3 will flash diagonally, and the whole rotation restarts only to the opposite directions.

Our *pregame talks* always began with an emphasis of the importance of F and F: *F*orcing passes (turnovers) and *f*ouls (sloppy defense). *This may seem oversimplified, but it is what dictates winning and losing in basketball.* At the pregame, before the players had entered the team room, I drew two large F's on the grease board. Beneath each F, I drew a single line downward to highlight some key words or thoughts about those game facets. For instance, under the first F, I might write in uncontested turnovers. Uncontested turnovers, because in our last game, we had too many of them. I might add a few reminders to discuss how these turnovers might be reduced. We might set a goal of a minimum number to work for that evening. I never liked to set minimum mistake goals. At the end of the game, you reflect back and notice you doubled that goal but annihilated the opponent. What then? An "I told you so" loses the bravado between you and your players. Your next lecture's appropriateness will have to be double accurate, and we know we don't want to enter that area.

Entering the gym for pre-game warm ups. If possible, follow the opponent's entrance. At away games, enter immediately following the opponent to come in to the opponent's rah's. Steal a little of their thunder. Good for your kids and displeases the opponents. At home, never come in before the opponent. If they wish to delay entering your gym to follow your entrance, all the better. It's your gym; all they are accomplishing is the valuable use of warming up in a strange gym with its strange background. Big mistake, big error. You don't need this gym exposure like your opponents. You know you have accomplished some success when the opponents watch your players enter. Watch for this: it is an interesting phenomenon. I have seen players stop what they are doing to watch our players run in, and it is not to admire the uniforms. Have your tallest players enter first, then as the shorter ones are entering, your tallest are slamming down a few dunks. Have your band play your entrance music annoyingly high. Anytime during pregame that the opponents leave the floor, take over the gym with some full-court drills. This is to your advantage. And when the opponents return, you are interfering in their court space, and you can then politely exit it.

Chapter 9

Managing the Game

Before entering the game with your team, it makes it easier on players if you quickly address their nerves. It is natural to be nervous before a contest, and you would be apprehensive about their preparedness if they were not edgy. Suffice it to say, "There is no valor without fear." So try to convert their nervousness to excitement. This is the time to turn off the lights in the room and take advantage of silence to get within themselves; advise them to imagine their success, to see their shots going in. We prayed silently as a team for a clean, safe game with no injuries. Thereafter, we, the coaches, kept the players active. After the pregame lecture and prayer, I would stand and high-five every player in the room. They would follow up and high-five every player. Much smacking going on. Pregame warm-ups . . . First drill should begin a few feet onto the opponents half of the court. Begin getting into their heads.

Once the game begins, settle down and be observant. What is happening? If you have a player that is making shots like he was shooting into a fifty-gallon drum, consider riding that horse. "An actual shooting phenomena that happens." Take the player out that seems like he couldn't hit the ocean from a row boat. This will demonstrate very honed coaching wisdom. Run many offensive and defensive plays in the first half; this gives your opposition a plethora of thoughts to discuss at halftime. For your advantage, remember what worked in the first half so that you might further exploit it in the second half. At halftime, keep to three topics of concern, no more. You might speak about opponents in foul trouble who, in the next half, will be restricted from playing tight defense. Maybe an opponent in the first half has drawn three fouls against himself; depending on the player, you may alternate the offense to better attack this player.

You might discuss both team's defensive flaws or strengths. You might discuss adaptations, mismatches, and switching defenders. Do not begin your half-time talk asking if anyone has any questions; rather, end the talk with time for questions. Your questions may have already been answered. You may have a few questions, such as "Does anyone need help on their man?" "Does anyone feel they have a favorable mismatch?"

Tempo control is important; know when to slow it down or run with it. *Start the game with an even press. (It's like taking the offense in a fight; you're getting in the important first punch.)* Wait for the opposition to call a strategy time-out, and then have your team change to an odd press. Watch the frustration in the opposition's coach as his time-out instructions crumble. For short periods, use a hard press and a zone press, and use a zone defense and a man-to-man defense and, if time permits, a gimmick defense all in the first quarter. And then maybe run a fake time-out? Memorize the opponent's countertactics. Run the second quarter accordingly. Take advantage in the second half of what you learned from the first half. You may need to tweak some schemes, but make adaptations few and simple.

Substituting. The coach or assistant must always speak to exiting players with positive words first and then enter corrections or suggestions if needed. All the fans are focused on a player exiting the game, so it is easy to embarrass that player by your actions as his coach. So take a deep breath, and handle the player as you would wish to be handled.

Don't say "don't" to your players. All that leaves on their minds is the possibility that they are going to do what you said "don't" to. It establishes a mental pressure or idea that might have been the last thought on their mind until then. As an example: you are stalling the ball and are in a team huddle defining the method of stall you are going to use. The last thing you want to leave with them is a negative statement such as "Now don't throw the ball away" or, even worse, "Listen, the only way we can lose this ball game is to rush our passes, so don't throw the ball away." A personal diatribe could not be any more counterproductive than "Tommy, are you trying to lose this game all by yourself? Don't throw any more bad passes!" A more appropriate and positive statement in the huddle would be better received and more constructive, such as "Let's make good passes. Let's pressure them into throwing the ball away."

Some games are lost not because of a substitute's abilities but because of their inattention at practice or on the game bench. The substitute's focus must be as intense as the starters for obvious reasons. To keep the bench personnel honed to the important aspects of the game, an important question might be asked to one of them rather than just the starters gathered. These questions will pay off. Besides keeping everyone involved in the game and aware of the immediate tactics needed, the entering substitute will be better prepared.

There are some players who think their only reason for joining a team huddle is to stretch a little. When dealing with youngsters with varied personalities and priorities, focusing on a single, common wavelength is—as best—horrendously wearisome. Some will be uninterested or just oblivious. I remember a player who had been in the game from the start. After a time-out where we have spent the entire time discussing and frantically drawing an intricate plan for that certain player to get open for the last shot, you hear—as the team breaks to go on the floor—that certain player whisper to a teammate with the question, "Whose ball is it?"

In a contest where wholesale substituting is appropriate, we—as a coaching staff—stumbled upon a fair system for getting this done. To get your remaining seven or eight players, who have had little or no playing time, equal substitute time, the following is useful, fair, and well received by the players. They enjoy the carousel, oscillating manner of substituting. They actually don't mind coming out, for no one has to sit but a short time with this musical-chairs rendition of alternating players. Your assistant coach can monitor the logistics. With every dead ball, you substitute one of your seven or eight players. The seating arrangement of the bench should look like below (S's being the starters and A through H representing your substitutes). Your S's, the starters, are out for the remainder of the game. (See illustration #24.)

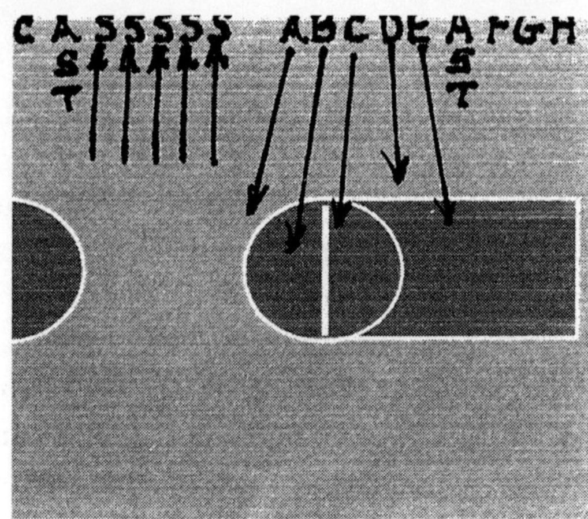

(24)

Your first substitution will be players A, B, C, D, and E. From then on, only one substitute at a time will enter. The first dead ball, A will exit and go to the end of the bench (where H is sitting), and F will enter. G and the rest of the reserves will slide over nearer the assistant coach. The next dead ball, B will exit and go to the end of the bench. G will enter, and H and the rest of the reserves will then slide over next to coach, and this rotation will continue through the end of the game. The synergy of this substituting method is very positive. Players are happy, and parents are happy. You will be surprised how many dead balls occur near the end of a game. Many do.

When a player comes out of the game, advise him to put his warm-up on. He will not be comfortable with this, but you want the player to maintain that heat for reentering.

Try to avoid matching up your best player with the opponent's hero.

A few comments on fast breaking. There is no better opportunity for your team fast-breaking than immediately after a fast break by your opponent to release your "Coast to Coast" offense. At that point, the opposition is unorganized and spread out the length of the court, and it is difficult to change directions as rapid as a fast break against oneself. So take advantage of their fast break against them. It works and if it's successful; it is as defeating to the opposition as being called for an offensive charge.

If you are playing a team that is an accomplished fast-breaking team, you can slow them down by defensively matching up personnel with the opponents that are defending you. Your conversion to defense is much quicker and can be made under the basket on the missed shot. To execute the fast break, it is important to rebound well. Thereafter, the fast break is reliant on ball control and verbal commands. The sideline release player or cherry picker is called upon to start the break with the verbal command "Outlet!" The possessor of the ball reacts to this command robotically, thus it is important that the release man is open for the pass. This trust and confidence in each other only appears after much verbal-cues practice. The inbounder or ball possessor, on hearing this command, can instinctively begin his outlet pass reaction. The next player further down the floor who is open asks for the pass by the command "Ball!" Your players must have no inhibitions about commanding loudly for the ball. A gym packed in attendance, including the band and cheerleaders, will create a din that makes verbal commands on the floor difficult to hear. Heaven forbid, one cannot imagine what will happen if the South African buzz makers, the vuvuzelas, catch on in America with our fans.

Read-Bounding

As coaches, we deter from using the term rebound and use read-bound instead. This emphasizes to our players the importance of first anticipating the correct angle of the rebound before attacking the basket. Old Newtonian science and the newer version of gravity by Einstein both dictate "what goes up will come down," so as a coach, you need to reassure this fact and then impose on your players to quit watching the ball's downward flight and find a man to screen out. The ball will come down. If you are coaching a very tall player, teach him to go to the ball; you do not want to waste that height out away from the basket, screening out some hobbit. I never coached screening out to a very tall player. Instead, I instructed them to go to the ball. All others, on inside position, I emphasized crossing their arms and leaning on their opponent. Having their arms crossed in front of their own body allowed them to extend one arm or the other once sensing the pressure of movement and direction. Extending that arm automatically places the backside of the arm to physically control and hold the opponent from his continued direction of pursuit of the ball. This gives the screener an improper advantage that myopic referees never recognize because it is wrongly assumed that you cannot hold with the back of the arm.

For the diminutive player caught among the behemoths under the basket, coach them to place the back of the hand on a tall chest and wait for the mistake that all tall players do: they will bring the ball down, which will be within your shorter player's reach for the steal or tie-up.

Free-Throw Screening

The inside defensive player should keep his arm higher than his opponent. On the gather step for jumping, the arm should be brought down over the opponent's arm for pinning the opponent to the ground. If the opponent is doing the same, then both hands should be kept high to stop quick, careening balls from passing over your head. Regards the footwork on free-throw rebounding, we were very strict. We gave our offensive players two moves they could select to use, but they had to use one of them. These moves practically nullified the opponent's inside position of advantage. The foot alignment, on the first move, was placing both feet together as close to the block as they could get. This position allows for a quick short step to cross in front of the opponent's outside foot. There is no rule that allows the inside person the right to the first step for screening out the opponent. The second move called for your player to stand as far away from the inside opponent as possible. For the opponent to screen out your player, he must move a good distance to make body contact. While this movement is occurring, your player assists him with a wraparound shove with the inside arm and swim-over move with the opposite outside arm. Presto! The inside position is now yours.

It is tough to coach a new move that has to eliminate an old habit, but if the player understands that his playing time is geared to his adhering to your little idiosyncrasies, his adaptation to your rules will be more readily used. What about slapping the shooter's hand after the free-throw shot? Why is that a no-no? We believe that nothing should come between the shot and the kinesthetic memory of the shot, especially a tingling in the shooting hand caused by two or three overzealous teammates congratulating and whacking the palm of the shooter. We would rather the last feeling the hand experienced was the release of the ball.

We used the sideline break to avoid the congested center court and to avoid the forced passes that seem to happen during the center fast break. It is important, when fast-breaking, to have a preponderance of players over the opponents. This is simply accomplished by requiring all players to break on every fast-break situation, regardless of their trailing positions. This is best established on the practice court by repeated and vehement style-breaking expectations. (See illustration #25.)

From the free-throw shot, we determined the fast-break side, on a controlled rebound, by the last number of the second-count on the game clock. If it is an even-number second, we break right; and if it is an odd-number second, we fast-break left. Of course, this is all predicated on an obliging rebound. If needed, at halftime, we may need to change our cue direction. (See page 123.)

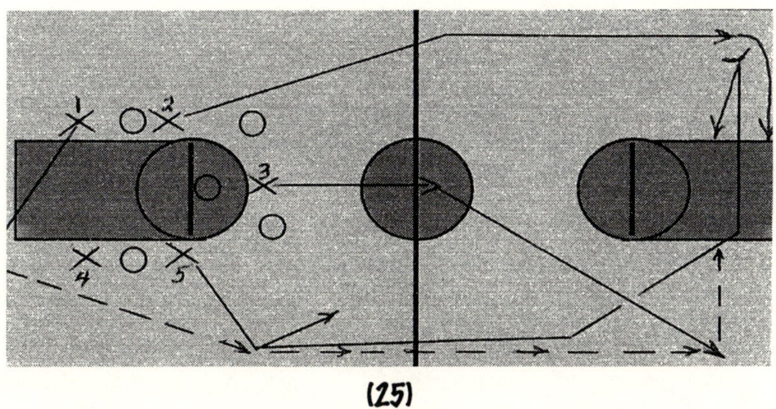

(25)

Eight seconds on the clock; all even-second times dictate a break down the right side of the floor. Your made-shot break begins with X1 taking the ball out-of-bounds and looking first for the long pass to a streaking teammate, possibly player X3. The next look and more common toss-in is to X4 or X5, both of whom are along the sideline giving outlet commands depending on the coverage. X3 is streaking down the court to the far baseline corner of the outlet. X3 then stations himself for a possible three-point shot based on the circumstances. X4 or X5, on receiving the outlet, read the coverage and determine whether to throw to X3 or dribble attack the defense. If the pass goes to X3, the passer cuts through the key, whether the defense is ahead of him or not. By this time, X2 is in the opposite corner, waiting for the cutter's screen. Your early offense can be easily adapted to this last option.

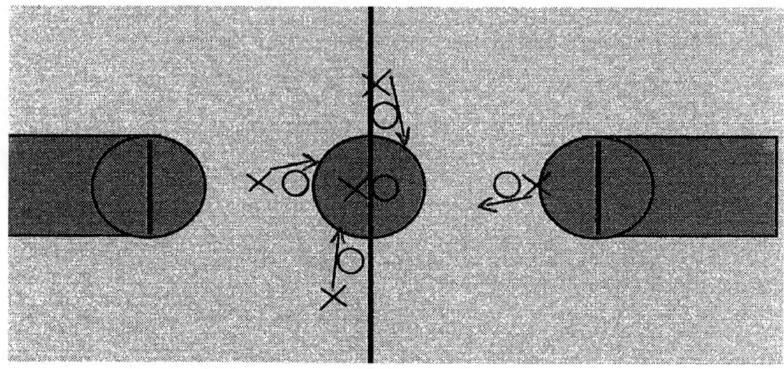

(26)

To ascertain a strong chance of recovering the tip on a jump ball, regardless of the height of your jumper, the above play is an equalizer. The O's are your opponents. Before the referee administers the toss, have your players stand immediately behind the opponents. This takes away any screens the opponents might have had in mind if you had joined them on the circle. On the referee's toss your players are going to shoot either right or left, determined by a call made from your team captain. On their shift, they slide onto the circle, right off the shoulder of their opponent. All four must slide in the same direction lest you will leave a quarter of the arc open to the opponents. Before the tip and the adjusted alignment, the jumper normally has already made up his mind who to tip to. This drives coaches crazy. If the jumper looks over the alignment, he first sees no advantages for the defense. However, he has no teammates side by side. When the jumper tips the ball, he does not know in what direction your team is coming or if you are even coming. You have a fifty percent chance of recovering the tip. (See illustration #26.)

The following is a simple but effective offensive tip-off play when you have height advantage. (See illustration #27.)

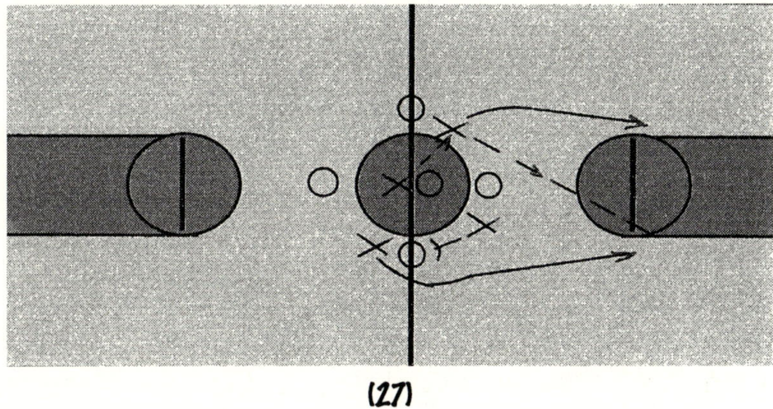

(27)

On the toss-up, the center jumper tips the ball to O3. O1 screens X5 from pursuing O2. O2 and O3, at the least, will have a two-on-one advantage over X4 to the basket. O2 may have a clear lane to the basket, with no one guarding him, and merely needs to receive a pass from O3.

Regards scouting, let the other teams worry about what you do. I believe it is more important to practice for all situations and forgo spending much time on scouting. Very few teams play the same games against others that they will play against you. Most teams match up differently against common opponents, and seldom do the same players have the hot hands against varied opponents. Your decision on scouting is yours, but I think all that is going to happen from a scouting report is that you are going to be inclined to change from something you have been working on all year. Information that is received from the media is probably as much information as you will need. In my early years, I traveled the road every free period that we were not playing or practicing to scout a future opponent. When I look back, I resent that time and money for what I received. I remember back to one opponent that I scouted three or four times. To make the story short, one player on this team never, never looked to score. I doubt that she ever knew where the basket was when on offense. Another player on this team handled the ball every time down the floor, and every offensive situation started with this player. What do you do with that information? Do you slide off the nonshooter and double deny the leader of the team? We met at the district finals. Their weak link shot five for six from the three-point line, and we squeezed out an overtime victory, no thanks to my scouting report—in fact, in spite of it. Maybe what I saw on these trips and what I synthesized from them was my erring. I, later, in years to come, saved on gas and spent more time with my team. Who knows? It's your decision.

Situations

Up by three points, little time left, seven or eight seconds, and the opponent has the ball. Do you foul him and send him to the line for one and one? He has to make the first shot, miss the second shot purposely, and get the rebound and put the shot back for two just to tie with you. That isn't going to happen!

You are shooting the second of a one-and-one free throw with three seconds to go in the game, and you are up by one. Miss purposely because the clock starts on the rebound, and there will be a short scrimmage under the basket. Make the shot, and the clock remains stopped, which gives time and life to the opponent.

Your hero is on the bench with four fouls. Near the end of the game, substitute him freely. Try to keep him out of the game while on defense and in the game while on offense.

A few seconds left, and a turnover creates possession to you. It's your lead; suck it up, and refrain from calling a time-out. I know the thought of time with your players to discuss the situations available will seem paramount to you, but you are stopping the momentum and giving the defense time to coalesce. I guarantee that if you allow the play to continue, the defense is going to do something proactive for your side. One thing I see continually in this situation is the defense double-teaming or chasing the ball, all to your advantage.

Properly use your team fouls, for no team wins a game in the first half. Relegate your starters with two fouls in the first half to the bench. If they are your heroes, then stall. Slow the game down for the remainder of the half. If the opponent does not come out after your spread-stall, fine. Sit on the ball. The opponents are making a huge tactical mistake.

A few last words about building a program. Keep your wins and losses in perspective. You must never let down on your coaching intensity because the truth is that your continued basketball future is in the decision-making hands and skills of seventeen—and eighteen-year-olds.

Tony Bush, Oregon's 2000 Assistant Coach of the Year, used to harmonize with me after a game that, "There is nothing like a win!" Maybe a big win? There are systematic changes that occur rapidly after a major win: (1) euphoria, (2) excitement, (3) exhaustion, and last, (4) satisfaction. Success is very personal; it is measured internally. Success is very self-satisfying; it brings peace of mind. However, you must expect raspberries intermingled with your roses in coaching.

It is difficult shaking off a bad loss—one where the game was very important or a night where your team played poorly. There is nothing more difficult than being crushed emotionally from a big loss and then having to stand in front of your team, sharing their pain and rationalizing the loss as a mistake, and then begin rebuilding their egos. I was more critical of my coaching than my cynics.

You can't walk away from a loss. The media will be on your coattail for an explanation of something they saw. They will pour salt on your wounds, wanting to discuss turnovers or poor shooting or your substituting judgment just minutes after the game is over. You will want to disappear, to just vanish. This personal contact with reporters is repugnant, for after a loss, you are reluctant to make eye contact with anyone, much less answer questions regards incidents that you are not sure why or how they occurred. The night after a loss is a late-television night. Trying to sleep is too agonizing because there will be nothing to interfere with memories of the game, over and over. There are systematic emotional stages that you can expect after a big loss. They are (1) depression, (2) anger, (3) self—and team—analysis, (4) optimism, and (5) a period of energization.

The first stages seem a little depressing, and they are. However, fortunately, in this profession, the highs far outweigh the lows. The first simile that comes to mind is that coaching is much like a roller-coaster ride. You will remember the exhilarating speed and the anticipation of feelings you had as you approached the first and highest summit of the ride, but you will forget the temporary upset stomach and lost items. So if you get the chance to enter this part of the game, take your Dramamine and zipper your pockets. You will enjoy the ride and especially those with you. Remember, it is just a game; there's no reason to take it so seriously that you lose its purpose—to have fun. Following is a picture of Coach Bush and myself donning our thinking caps in warm-ups for an important game.

Regards this chapter, "Managing the Game," my best friend and wife, Bette, has successfully managed the character above for forty-plus years, sat through countless games and road trips, shared the pain, and soothed my brow over the losses, while raising three children. She has always managed her critiques of my games painlessly but usually "correct and direct." She also has been the efficient manager of our household. She also proofread this book. You are probably thinking she should have written it. She should have.

Chapter 10

Gimmick Plays and Tricks

I believe in gimmick plays, especially with defenses, but only when they are applicable and are not coached at the expense of too much practice time. A gimmick defense, too seldom used in high school, is the box-and-one. I do not use the box alignment because when we run a zone defense, it is regularly out of the one-three-one alignment. So to use the practicality of the box-and-one, we adapt it to out 131 zone. This makes the new defense very simple to run and to teach. Our players still execute their zones as before, except for the point defender. He no longer has a zone area to cover. Some teams will free up the defender in the zone that the opponent's hero sets up in. Then all helps must shade to that zone. We found it simpler to use our point defender for four reasons: (1) because that zone is the furthest from the basket and easiest to help cover, (2) because the defender of that zone is usually one of our quickest and ablest man-to-man coverers, (3) because we are not losing a rebounder with that match-up, (4) because quite often, the opponents hero sets up business in that zone area.

We call this defense the "thirty-one chase." It is not designed by Armani, but it fits our defense well. The chaser has a very demanding job, but a simple one. All emphasis on this position is deny. Its only role is to chase the hero and deny him from receiving a pass. It is tiring on the chaser and the pursued. That advantage goes to the defense, for we can freely substitute our chasing defender.

The flaw in this defense is that the hero can post up in a low-post zone area. The offensive player that was there before the post-up can leave. This leaves two defenders on the hero: the player assigned to that zone area and the chaser. The offensive player that left is now free of a defender and can overload another zone. This offensive move is also successful against a triangle-and-two defense. The two in the triangle-and-two are man-to-man defenders chasing two high-scoring offensive players. As above, if you send those two heroes down to the low-post areas and pop out the offensive players assigned to those areas, you now have four defenders guarding your two scorers down low. This leaves you with three offensive players against one defender above the free-throw line and extended. The only time I ever used the triangle-and-two defense was against two excellent scorers whose cast also included three players who couldn't hit space from a satellite.

I don't believe it's fair to call a defense that is executed correctly a gimmick play. If the rotations are sound and they don't present unusually difficult situations to cover, it seems to me to be just another defense. Early kibitzers of the matchup zone probably now practice it and exhort it to others.

The "Open Trap" or half-court trap is a favorite surprise defense, one that is seldom run continually. It is an exhausting defense that calls for much sprinting and for much rabid trapping. It is an ideal defense for changing tempo or for creating chaotic offensive confusion. A prime time for this attacking defense is the last minute or two of each quarter. The defense has no zone principles, nor does it qualify as a man-to-man defense. Interested? Your first defender sets up in the middle of the court at the midcourt line. Your two wing defenders are originally placed approximately 9 feet deeper than your middle defender and approximately 10 feet inbounds from their respective sideline. Your remaining defenders are placed in the general area of the free-throw elbows. All initial setups are to discourage inner passes. The first trap can occur anywhere on the half-court perimeter. Ideally, the first attempted pass should be up high between their guard and wing, and that is promotable. (See illustration #28.)

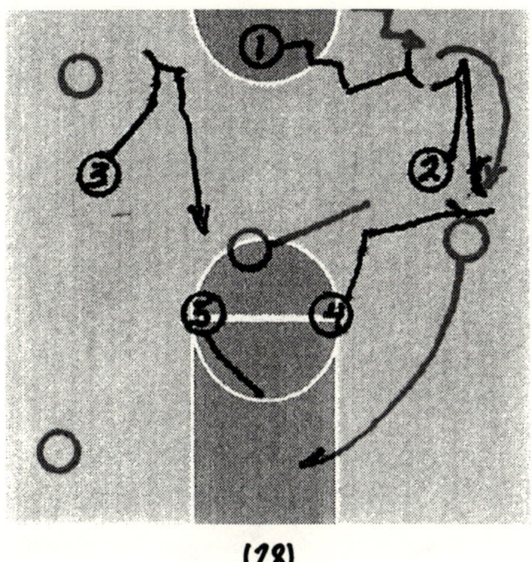

(28)

Roles

Your first defender should be tall and quick, but not a necessity. His role is to meet the offensive player while still in control of his dribble. He needs to slow the dribbler enough that the dribbler is looking for a receiver to pass to. With the aid of a wing defender who overplays his offensive man, your first defender can force the lob pass back to the open wing. Most likely, one of your wing men will be the initial trapper with your first man. Your post defenders are frantically denying passing lanes to deep personnel, with exception to the far diagonal receiver from the ball.

Rules

Force passes around the perimeter. Do not allow drivers to the center. Gamble on stealing all perimeter passes.

Rotations

You will notice in the diagram above that X4 and X3 are not hard denying their receivers O3 and O2. The purpose being we want slow lob passes that are challengeable by weak-side help. You can vary this by having X4 and X3 smothering their receivers; it all depends on your respective talent.

If O1 was to break the trap with a dribble to the left, X2 would follow to trap again with the aid of X4. X1 would cover the first man from the ball up high. X5 would cover the first man from the ball down low. X3 would drop to, center field, the original spot of X5, looking for defensive players two passes away from the ball. If O1 was to break the trap with a pass to O3, all rotations would be the same as above.

If O1 was to break the trap with a dribble to the right, X1 would follow to trap again with the aid of X3. X5 would cover the first man from the ball toward the wing. X2 would cover the first man to the ball in the opposite direction of the dribble. X4 would drop to, center field, the original coverage area of X5, looking for receivers two passes away. If O1 was to break the trap with a pass to O2, all rotations would be the same as the break by dribble.

If the opponents break this second trap, you continue to trap with the same rotational principles of above. All your players must understand that it is beneficial to them to cut the floor in half and force play on the strong side.

Tips

Before you apply this defense, ascertain that your players are up to it physically. To play it correctly, your defenders must fly from position to position and trap to trap. Possibly the time for a wholesale substitution with players that have spent extra time in practice with this defense. Call them your trap specialists. They will appreciate that recognition. With fallible high school players, expect some confusion on second and third traps. Do not be discouraged with this confusion; it still commits the opponents to turnovers.

Wrong-Way-Play Gimmick

If it's your possession right after halftime, attempt the wrong-way-play. You never have anything to lose. First, discuss with the referee what you will be doing so he doesn't inadvertently tip off the play to the opposition by being overhelpful. You have heard the story of the referees on a walk, arguing over tracks, whether they were deer or bear. The argument was settled abruptly as a locomotive ran over them. This parody grossly makes fun of the eyesight of referees, but it does illustrate that there probably must be a need to guide these gentlemen. So advise these nearsighted souls of the intent of the wrong-way-play trick, or sure enough, they will foul it up. They are supposed to referee, not coach. So if they know that you know what you are doing, they will keep quiet, or they should. The play develops as follows: the whole team lines up for the ball in the wrong court, opponents will follow like sheep, then a designated player sprints to the opposite and correct end for the uncontested lay in. Don't expect a coach-of-the-year vote from the opposing coach, especially if you convert on the play.

A *stall play* is where your players don't have to play at the speed of light to slow time. It is also easier than general relativity for your players to learn. This stall requires no dribbling; it removes small quick defenders from your exchanges and can be used as a last-minute shot offense or a play designed to sit on the ball with crossed legs, watching the time run down. In a close game with little time remaining, your players must be convinced that the enemy is no longer the opponent; the enemy has become the game clock. For your opponents, the time ticking down is becoming your sixth player. So take advantage of these numbers and milk this time. (See illustration #29.) Consider a situation where you have a one-point lead, one minute to go, and a lay in presents itself. Do you take it or stall? If you take it and make it, you still leave the outcome of the game in the opponents' hands. They go down and hit the three, and you lose. If you had stalled with the lead, likely, they would have had to foul. Now you hit the free points, and they must go down and hit the three with less time than they had before? I think if you study this stall and practice it, you will be amazed by the secure control it gives you and the offensive options it provides; however, you do not want those, right? We called this play "Victory," I guess, as a subliminal message to our team that we, as in baseball, are sending in our best relief pitcher to end the game. We have beat the opponent; now let's beat the clock. You could see the confidence play in our players increase when they heard the command to run Victory from the bench.

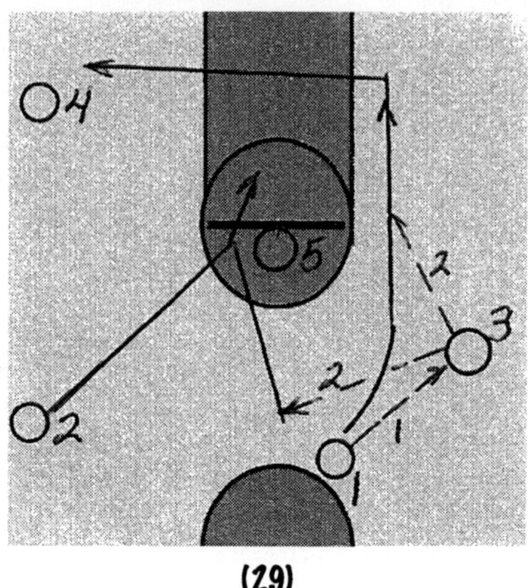

(29)

Roles

O3 will be your primary ball handler. He needs to be strong, possibly your team's best player or athlete. O5 is primarily in a release valve-type position. O1, O2, and O4 should be your best passers and/or ball handlers.

Rules

One of the requirements of this stall is no one is standing still, like most stalls. It gives the impression that you are trying to score. You could. *(I have often toyed with this stall as a team offense. It would probably do well. It's just not in my nature for the long run, for I prefer the quick-hitter's game.)* O5 posts up on the midpoint of the free-throw line or somewhere on the left side, removed from O3. O4 is diagonally far removed from O3. O1 is in your typical position for a point guard, and for the illustration above, he has the ball. O2 is at a high wing perpendicular from O3.

Rotations

O3 makes a downward move to open himself back at his starting spot. O1 makes a good pass and hits O3, coming back to his original spot. Following the pass, O1 cuts to the basket for a lay in or to show the threat of same. At the same time, O1 cuts to the basket O2 has cut down to O5 for the screen or threat of same. Once he gets to O5, he cuts back to the point position where he gets a safe pass from O3. Earlier, at the same time O2 cuts for O5, O4 slides up to O2's old position. O1 is still cutting under the basket to O4's old position, and the team's rotation goes on. While this carousel continues, O5 is keeping mobile in the confines of his position while always begging for the ball. Every time O3 receives the pass, he has the option of hitting O1 on his cut or calling for O5 to screen him or just driving on his own or passing back to the point, coming off of O5's screen. After a few laps of this stall, with all its motion, you can anticipate the defense is going to anticipate steals, which will permit you some very creative cuts and passes, especially to O3. At the least, this stall allows you simple, short passes back and forth between the offensive spots of O1 and O3. The movements of your other players deny the defense from double-teaming and requires them to stay spread. Imagine the looks O2 can get from continued cutting off of O5 to the basket. Yet lest we forget, we are stalling for the win or last shot. It's difficult to coach your players not to pull the trigger early; however, maybe, you will not want to. A bonus to this stall is there is no dribbling necessary.

The three-point shot is not a difficult shot to set up during regulation time. Drive the ball, attack the basket from different angles, and you can pop the ball back out for a good three-point look; but near the end of the game and when the opposition does not fear the two-point shot, the three-point look becomes extremely difficult. To get a favorable three-point look, you must manipulate the defense into a help situation or screen off an opponent. After a few hard skip passes you will see whether the opponent is going to fall into a help-side trap. When the opponent is too smart to play help-side defense, you must rely on a multiscreen offense. My favorite is the deep corner fake. (See illustration #30.)

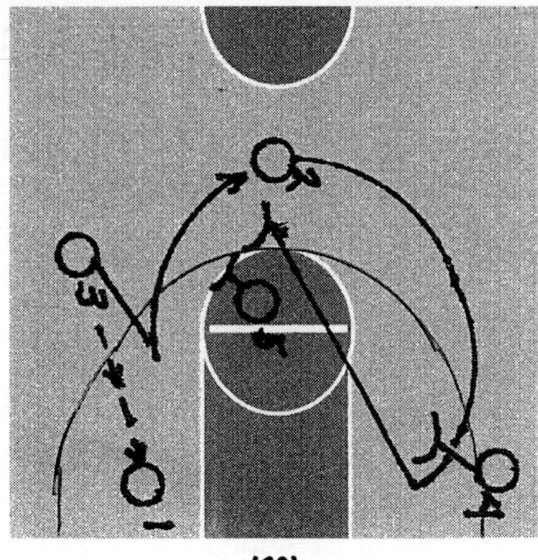

(30)

O2 shoots towards the opposite side of the floor in the direction of the opposite corner off of O4's screen; rather than continuing this route, O2 curls around O4 in the direction of the top of the key, at which point O2 and O5 set up a double screen high in the key near the three-point line. While this is occurring, O1 who has the ball looks toward O4 who is now on the three-point line in the corner. After this quick feinting move toward O4, O1 skips a pass to O3, coming off the double pick. The same play can be used, time allowing, without the feinting pass to O4 from O1. Instead, O1 just throws from his position to O3 and flashes to the strong side of the double pick by O2 and O5 to set a pick for O2. Once O3 has the ball and looks for O2 coming off the triple screen, it is likely that O4's defender will loosen to help with the high-point action and leave O4 uncovered for an option skip pass and three-point look.

Handling Referees

You should

1. call them by their first names.
2. never look them in the eye, unless you are complimenting them on a call. It is amazing what one can say without seeming confrontational when there is no eye contact.
3. stay seated if you are venting.

Supplied with this above information, you would think that I knew better than the following: I had noticed that a female referee had on very high, high-water-length official pants. They probably came halfway up her shins, not so far that her socks still didn't cover her legs. In thirty years of coaching basketball, I probably had, at the most, ten technicals called against me. I was never removed from a game. I was having a frustrating night and did not believe she was involved enough when I bellowed out at her, "Why don't you pull those pants down and blow your whistle?" Oops, the connotation came to me quickly on what she thought I meant. I certainly did not mean for her to blow it out her—. To compound the situation, I probably made the cardinal sin of looking into her eyes when I spoke. She became the embodiment of a referee in control. I became the coaching paragon of how one should not act toward a referee. The result was a technical foul. I did not try to argue her call.

Fun with referees?

Time-out and your free throw shooter is being iced:

1. On a one minute time-out, can your shooter spend the time-out on the floor with one of your team's ball, practicing free throws?
2. On a one minute time-out, can your shooter play catch out-of-bounds with a teammate, simulating free-throw shooting, outside the team huddle?

Before a legal dribble begins and with both feet planted where the pivot foot has not yet been established, may the player bounce the ball with both hands off the floor without making any foot advancement? The rule book states he can touch the floor with the ball and return it to an upright position repeatedly without advancing.

Can a shooter go up on the lay in, through the basket, and release the ball above the rim and let it fall down through? When he dunks it, his hands are over the cone. Another question, why would he want to?

On the end line, the tosser is regulated on how deep he may stand. Ask ten referees how deep the tosser can be out-of-bounds on a sideline pass. Ask the same ten whether an inbounds pass must be free of a player or any player's physical contact with the ball. In other words, can it be handed by the tosser if he hands it over the plane or invisible wall from across the line?

Light moments with referees?

Are you less likely to receive a technical foul if you pass on a thought to the referee, i.e., "Our coach thinks (not says) your calls are worse than your decision to become a referee."

As I said earlier, handling referees requires learning their first names, thus it behooves you to write them down before the game starts. During your periodic mild heated exchanges of viewpoints with the referee, make no visual contact—especially and absolutely no second looks. You can safely vent yourself and demean the referee while staring at the cheap seats. Be diplomatic when questioning a call. An example of how politeness will work to your advantage is when you question a disputed call by frantically exchanging with the referee about your better view: "No, no. I saw it! The other player pushed first, sir!" When handled in this manner, you are likely to hear the referee tell the official scorer, "I'm sorry. The coach says he had a better vantage to see the play, so change the foul to the other player. Thanks, Coach!"

Most referees are dumfounded when you react to a questionable call by sending three players out to play a zone defense on the opponents and two to guard the referees man-to-man. The referees will deserve an explanation for this tactic. Your response, "We always play man-to-man on the people hurting us the most" will endear yourself with the fans but sever any further communicating with the referees. I do not recommend this action unless—of course—the game is lost and it is the season finale.

Physically impeding the referee by jumping on the court and testing his whistle is always a light moment that sometimes ends up being helpful. Stay away from "The other referee is laughing at your calls" comment. It might be a momentary and satisfying stress reliever, but you never know their relationship to each other. A favorite equalizer is when the referee is at the opposite end of the floor and he gives you a favorable call. You loudly berate him; he is not going to think it came from your bench and will cast the stink eye at your opposing coach.

Never admit a turnover or error. For example, do not ever quit your dribble on an obvious error that you have made. Sometimes, a referee will change a collision foul to the opponent; but because of your action, he might reverse what he was about to call. Teach your teams to clap and celebrate contested balls that have gone out-of-bounds to influence the decision. Instead of giving up an over-and-back rolling ball, follow it without touching it and stay close enough to fight over it when the opponent attempts to pick it up. The automatic turnover becomes a jump ball. Don't expect clever comment remembrances from the stripes until later down the years.

I remember a first-year varsity high school coach in Southwestern Oregon who lost his first game due to a single referee call, or he thought so. After the game, before the referee in question disappeared to the basement dressing room, which at that gym is the same as the hereafter, this coach made hot pursuit to cut him off from the basement door. To question this referee before he got to the "black hole," the coach used the Pythagoras's theorem to cut him off. To do so, and follow the hypotenuse, it required him to leap the ticket table. A tacky move, so it should have ended there. Like John Wilkes Booth, he caught his heel and without a peep of "Sic semper tyrannis" stumbled and caught himself with his hands wrapped around the referee's neck; it was a self preserving reaction, I'm sure, but was completely misunderstood by the departing fans.

The next morning, in school, the coach was summoned to the principal's office.

The conversation, over something that the coach thought was already settled, was one-sided. The principal said, "You are going over to the opposition's school and make an apology to their student body. It has already been organized for you. You are then to find the home of the referee that you accosted and personally apologize to him." After the school assembly debacle, the coach located the referee's home, who was a minister, and was refused entry without a police officer present. Once abided, the coach returned to his school and continued to coach there for many controversial years. A different man? Nope, just a first chapter. Could happen to anyone? I don't think so. This coach went on to win a few and lose a few over his career, but his games always drew packed gyms.

Unfortunately, most coaches believe you must constantly be riding the referees during a game lest the opposition receives more favorable calls.

It has become part of the game. Do not provoke the referees when you have the ball. If you feel that a technical is needed, create it when the opponent has the ball. Most coaches know when to let up or increase their berating of the referees. Most coaches continue their criticisms right up to the edge of a technical. I bring this up because of the importance of your bench keeping silent toward the calls. You know when to stop, you know when you are close to the last straw . . . If a player from the bench or an assistant makes a comment, it is given to the head coach. Many a coach has been disqualified and removed from a game for a minor comment from a player on the bench. Player bench decorum must be coached and monitored.

The game of basketball has become more physical over the years. Coaches teach this physical play lest their teams succumb to the aggressiveness of their opponents. Prepare your teams for the extra contact in playoffs and especially state tournament games. Referees that are voted in for postseason work are allured by extra pay for what could be considered semiretirement efforts. There has become a reluctancy to make game-changing calls. A "let them play the game" dictates the calls, especially the late ones and in the big games.

Opposing Coaches

Do not allow them to have private time with their players during the game; send over a spy. I coached my players to listen in if the opposing coach called over one of his players for a tete-a-tete. Whoever from my team was the closest to the situation would walk right over and lend an ear. This stranger's presence always caught the opponent's coach by surprise and immediately silenced him.

Do not call your time-outs while your player is in control of the ball along the sideline or in the backcourt. It is much more simple to score from under your own basket, on an inbound toss, than it is from 30 feet away. So call your time-outs with instructions to your team to always take the ball to your baseline and then call time-out. Do this with a coded call so that the referee doesn't react to your action and stop play before your player can advance the ball to your baseline. Just before calling a time-out, check the opponents' bench. They may be harboring the same thought and unsuspectingly accommodating you by calling their time-out before you and saving you a time-out; it happens and often.

Player Contracts

Determine and share your points of interest with your team. My method of addressing them was by player-coach contracts. My last team was weak on following shots and didn't look enough for charges to suit me. So I contracted with the team that for every successful put back or successful charge taken in a game or practice, that player was rewarded with an "Earnie." Every Earnie awarded could be turned, in exchange, into sitting out a conditioning drill. Earnies could be amassed and carried forward to the next year. They could be given or sold to other players. The interesting things about Earnies were they were seldom used. Most players would save their Ernies, worrying that a future conditioning drill may be worse, and elect to retain their Earnie. I have past players who still have unused Earnies. Earnies have always worked out to be very productive for improving team weaknesses. In retrospect, when I use this ploy in the future, I should make the Earnie a physical object that is a tasty edible award. What was I thinking?

Sweet Sixteen Operational Gimmick Notes

1. Regard to last second plays, especially in overtime, make them driving plays. Referees tend to react closer to defensive fouls on drivers when the game is late; in addition, defenders are shy from fouling and will play passive on the shot.
2. Remember that defenders tend to relax when the offensive player they are guarding passes the ball. This gives the offensive player a split-second advantage for using a ballistic move.
3. A simple play versus a man-to-man defense is to ask for a pass from your teammate by extending your arm and open hand out as a target. Rather than an open hand, close it to a fist. This is to advise the tosser not to pass it but to fake the pass. Then with the aid of an arm-over swim move right at the

time your teammate fakes you that pass, you cut for a backdoor lay in pass. This is a play with high-percentage results; you just can't use it too often.

4. Obviously, if you have a referee's child playing in this game, you call on that player to . . .
5. When do tactics become unethical? Do you rehearse injury time-outs and supply a simple code to the team for when and who will execute the feigned injury (such as shouting out, "Tommy, fall down!")? A more sophisticated code might sound like "Three!" However, you better have a player assigned to fall; otherwise, you will end up seeing five players writhing in pain on the floor.) One contest, an opposing coach obviously used two extra time-outs with this method. Then tackily, he raised his last injured player from the bench to reenter and hit the game-winning basket. It was a miracle? I was too emotionally involved to complain?
6. On last-second fouls, coach your players that this foul should be more than a gesture but a real legitimate effort for the steal.
7. When you need to foul intentionally to stop the clock during an inbounds pass, foul any man; this does not have to be the man receiving the ball. Also, think about fouling while the ball is out-of-bounds and the clock is stopped; but you need to make certain it is unintentional, just rough enough to be noticeable. Grabbing the jersey to stop or direct the opponent's motion should suffice.
8. Don't allow a three-point shot to tie you when you are up by three points with little or no time left. Foul *before* the opponent attempts the shot; no one purposely or successfully converts an attempted missed free throw.
9. When your opponent is working for a last shot, remember to use your team fouls when under the bonus situation. Example: The game is within forty seconds of being over. If you burn your fouls correctly, you might run the time down, which will cause your opponent to have to rush their play or shot attempt.
10. Attempt last shots with at least seven-seconds on the clock, no later. This gives you some put-back time and adjusts for your players starting the shot too late.
11. When the opponent is down by one or two and has possession, hold from fouling until there are about twelve seconds remaining on the clock. The team in possession is under the most pressure and will tend to make turnover mistakes as the clock ticks down.

12. In the first half, substitute your players out that have two fouls. If they are really important to the team and will be noticeably missed, slow it down or stall until you can reenter them after halftime. In overtimes, remind your outside shooters to aim for the back of the rim. Their tired legs are going to cause their shots to be short.
13. After a successful lay-in, an opportune time for a steal quite often presents itself. The shooter now charges back downcourt to set up for defense. His direction should be toward the closest and most likely opponent to receive the inbounds pass. On his second step, his back still to the player throwing the ball in, he plants and pivots with his hand extended in what he feels will be the passing lane. The offensive player, seeing this defensive player's back to him, sometimes becomes too casual with the toss-in and allows it to be stolen. If the toss-in by the opponent is a controlled one, the shooter, instead of seeking the steal, sets up behind the potential receiver and takes the charge on his reception step.
14. Teach your players that during time-outs, if you assemble in a circle near the floor, the starters have their backs to the floor. This makes it much easier on the coach who is instilling a point or an idea to see his player's eyes. Whether your team stands or sits during a time-out, make certain all their personal needs are taken care of in the first ten seconds of the time-out. This gives you their full attention when you begin to speak . . . if you have anything to say . . .
15. Coach your offensive players on how to drag a low-post defender who is in foul trouble. After receiving the low-post pass, a strong pivot squaring up to the basket is normally recommended. However, when your offensive-post man is backing in with the ball and sees an extended arm over his shoulder to the ball side, a scoop shot (underhanded lay in) will draw the foul, with the follow-through of the shooting arm coming up under the arm of the defender.
16. Coach your players on how to avoid "floppers." These are players who extend their ball-side leg during the shot to make contact and then fall backwards at the slightest touch. Know who these players are, and defend them straight up without any forward jumping or reaching. Some of these players are also adept at flopping on lay ins. Again, keep your arms back demonstratively for the referees' benefit. Floppers usually lose out by their inability to garner second shot attempts.

Five offensive inbounds plays to live by:

1. (Versus a man-to-man defense) The rule book reads that if you are three feet or more from the baseline and have established position, you cannot be moved from that position. Interpreting this to your advantage means that all four of your players can nestle together (see illustration #30) and run a play from that position. This is my favorite inbounds play when I have at least one tall player. We call the play "Cube." Our players line up back-to-stomach and side-by-side with no space between them. Defensive players are not allowed inside them or between them. The opponents are relegated to a perimeter defense. The execution of the play begins with O2, O3, and O5 crossing their arms, elbows up, throat high. Players O2, O3, and O4 then expand the cube by taking one short step forward, leaving a pocket for O4 to step into and jump to catch the inbounds lob, followed with a simple lay in. Seems too easy; it is easy and works so simply.

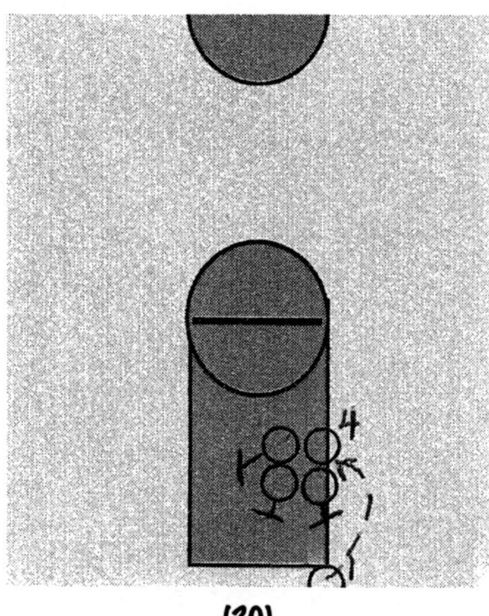

(30)

Cube executed against opponent. In the picture below, our players arms are beginning to raise neck-high. They then will step forward, presenting a pocket for our post person to step into.

David Angyal, Anthony Godlove and Michael Crocker defend the inbounds play.

If we have a better pin available than using the screens for O4, we simply call out another teammate's nickname. The other players in the cube fan out to leave the player called with a defender on his back. (See illustration #31.) It would be player O5 that was called. The other potential receivers would charge up toward the cheap seats, leaving O5 with an easy step forward, with his defender on his back. It works. If the tosser's defender was overhelping on the play, our tall receiver would not catch the ball but merely tap it back to the tosser who had quickly come inbounds to be a legal receiver just under the basket. So easy a play that the opponent's fans will loudly claim their displeasure—most of them about the legality of the play. Sweet!

(31)

basket
O
X
XX
O2O3
O4O5
X

2. (Versus a man-to-man defense) Height does not matter. We line up our receivers on the four corners of the free-throw area. For you old-timers and traditionalists, the corners of the key. We call the play "Spider" for no better insect. (See illustration #32). On a command, the far diagonal players quickly trade places. That means four offensive players running to opposite corners at exactly the same time. With four defenders, this creates a potential concussion group of eight. To execute Spider correctly, all four players meet in the center at the same time. This is the crux of this assembled web. They then have to kick, scratch, and head-butt through this pileup to advance to the other corner. I tell my players, if they are chipping teeth and scraping knees and finishing the play with a limp, they were probably executing Spider correctly. The main problem to Spider, besides keeping players, is coaching your passer to wait on the inbound toss. Coach your passer to have patience; in another split second, someone else might appear without a defender, a defender probably never to be seen again. Often after my games were over, the referees who remembered this play would ask me to please diagram it for them. I never did on paper; it would seem to be too ridiculously simple to work, for it was the kamikaze execution that made it successful, plus it would make me appear to be some sort of Bohemian coach. To moderately sophisticate the chaos of this play, because you never know who will pop open, suppose you could focus certain players to mass screen one person's man. But the mass collision method seemed to work the best and was most entertaining to watch. Just remember to be patient on the toss-in. Not a good play for setting up your best free-throw shooter to receive the ball. Your receiver is totally out of the control of coach and toss-in player.

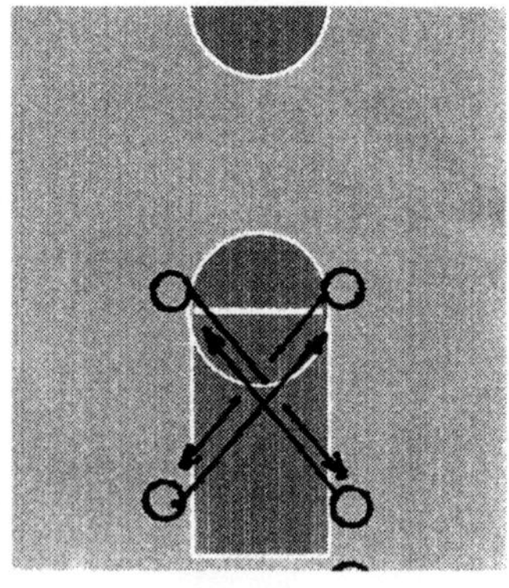

(32)

3. (Versus a man-to-man press) (See illustration #33.) Shade your primary receivers to the side of the toss-in man. His defender will be shading him to the inside to use the backboard as a defender against the long toss to the opposite side, thus his hands will be down to stop the shorter pass to that opposite side. They must be, assuming that he is playing up man-to-man on the tosser. Send two players deep to the backcourt to spread the defense. On play action, one of these players will be designated to sprint back along the sideline, past the midcourt line, toward the toss-in man to help the passer's options. The two primary receivers in the front court should be set up, about the distance of the free-throw area width apart, but back about 6 feet past the free-throw-shot line. This gives the primaries more room to work in, especially while coming back to the tosser. Ideally, the reception should occur, when coming towards the passer, at about *8 to 10 feet from the base line***.** Heaven forbid a pass in to one of your receivers close to the baseli1ne. A definite no-no! You're adding to the cardinal rule of "Are you kidding me?" An instant turnover—just add water! You want the reception to occur at the depth of about the free-throw line. Any other type of reception should be covered in rice. The primary screen between O2 and O3 is dictated by the side of the basket the toss-in player is planted. As illustrated above, O2 would initiate play by back screening O3's defensive man. Once the screen was set, O3 would feint toward the toss -in player and then streak down the floor toward O5 but not as far as the midcourt line. O2 is pinning the defensive man from the ball and breaking to the toss-in player, with his defender on his back. O3 has now stopped abruptly and returned to set a screen for O2 who should have the inbounds pass. (This screen is not meant to create switching confusion, however very acceptable, but to be a charge-taking type of screen. There is little in basketball as devastating as an offensive charge.) O4 is in a read position still coming to the toss-in player for outlet support. *Dribble advancement should never be in the direction of a teammate.* The dribbler should be looking for open space, not for a buddy. Advancing toward a teammate with your defender and your teammate's defender being put in proximity increase the chances for a turnover. The offense must try to make the defense cover as much floor as possible. No more than three players should be in a half court at a time.

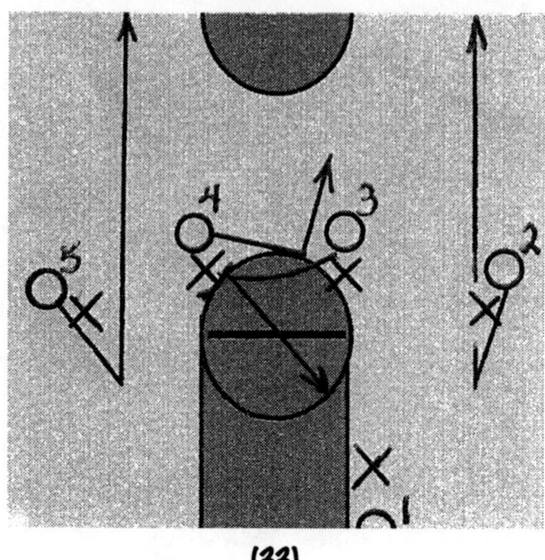

(33)

4. (Versus an even zone defense) This play takes some practice because there are no assigned places for each player, thus everyone needs to know all of its movements. (See illustration #34.) O5 will be the primary lay in shooter; however, O3 will often be open for the three-point shot. O4 often gets a simple 15-foot look and O2, a power lay in. The play begins with three simultaneous movements. O2 will post up low, pinning out X1 from the basket and drawing X2 over to deny the simple inbounds pass. O3 kicks out to the far corner for the three and/or to draw out X3. A tunnel opens up between X2 and X3. At this time, O5 has flashed over to post a fake screen on X4 or at minimum to freeze X4 in that zone. At this time, O5 fakes coming off the screen and shoots back down the tunnel. After passing the ball to O3, O1 comes back on the playing court to pin the helping X2 from stopping O4's shot. Once learned, it is beautiful to watch this play's operation. All movements should be choreographed to occur at one time, with the exception of the inbounder's screen, which has to happen after his pass in to O3. We run many of these half-court inbounds plays because when our players call a time-out, they never do so in the backcourt. They always take the extra time to drive the ball to the baseline before calling "time." Why not? It is so much simpler to score from your baseline than it is from the side-court line. Um?

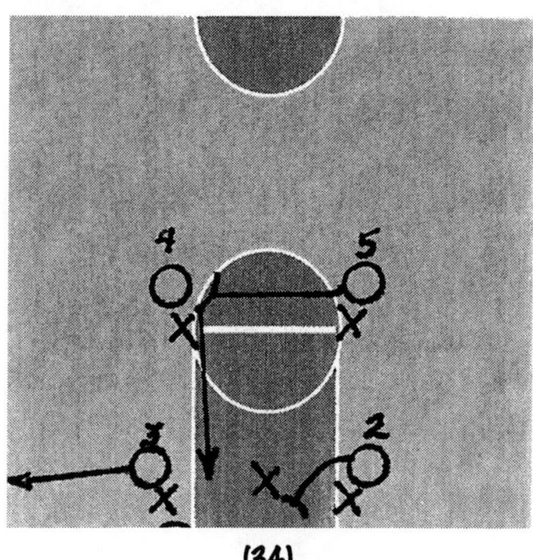

(34)

5. (Versus a panic press) Meaning there are only a few seconds left in the game and the opponents are denying passes because they are down by only a point or two. This play will keep you from sleeping later, because it is so like taking candy from six-foot babies. You set up the player O1 who is tossing the ball in as far back off the inbounds line as possible to nullify a tall person harassing his inbounds toss. O3 and O4 are set up between the midcourt line and the free-throw line extended. O2 and O5 are posted on the free-throw line, extended near the side lines. O1 is your team's best passer. O2 and O5 are your quickest players; if you are concerned with only getting the ball in safely and not trying to draw a foul, then you should look for shooters for these positions. O3 and O4 are tall and have good hands. On command, O2 and O5 come towards O1 with both hands out for the reception. They take one step only; and then both of them—with an outside arm swim-over move—fly straight down the floor, for they are the primary receivers. Your secondary receivers now are O3 and O4. Both of these receivers are going to take two fake steps toward O1 and then stop, pivot, and ask for an alley-oop pass to their outside extended hands. This does not have to be a touch pass, for the defenders have to be in denial positions; and if the alley-oops are lobbed too far, there will be no one there to intercept, with O2 and O5 under the opposite basket by now. (See illustration #35.)

The last time my team ran this play was under an identical situation. There were three seconds on the clock. We are not in the bonus. We are playing that year's eventual state champions. We are up one, and I position our all-league quarterback to toss in the lob pass. An accurate long lob could be intercepted, and we would still win. The play begins, and O2 has a five-foot lead on his defender. My quarterback winds up and tosses an errant pass over both benches into the cheerleaders' victory formation, which was being prematurely assembled for our win. The same quarterback, who on the football field could wedge the ball into a facemask on deep passes, misses the entire basketball court from no distance away. The ball touches no one on the floor, so the opponents gleefully get the ball under their own basket with three seconds to run a play. I have to tell my managers to sit down; they are gathering our extra balls for the trip home.

The thrill of victory to the agony of defeat in three seconds. The opponents win. Under extreme duress, which excuses one in court from guilty actions, I told my quarterback that he was as far off from receiving a passing grade in my Personal Finance class as he was on that pass. I would run the same play again if I had to do it over. Yes, even with the same failing, knuckle-headed quarterback.

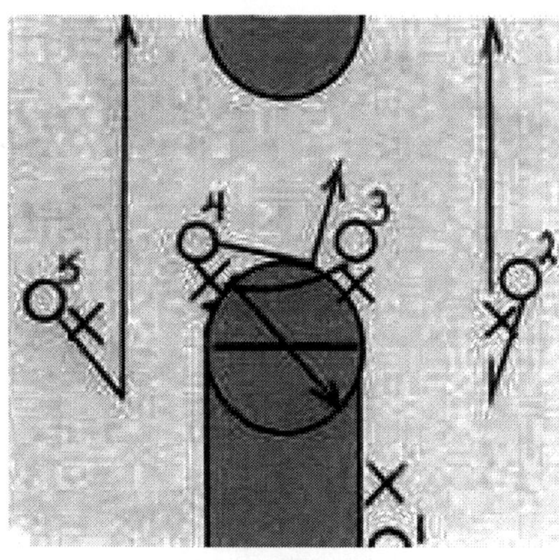

(35)

An inbounds play not to live by. But one I have, over the years, become increasingly attached to. Here is an inbounds under-the-basket play that causes duress in defensive coaches and their players. This was the only play we summoned by a color. So it had many names: purple, violet, green, which we gleefully changed each time we called the play. We set up a side-by-side tandem two feet inside the free-throw line. Our receivers' shoulders made tight contact. (See illustrations below.)

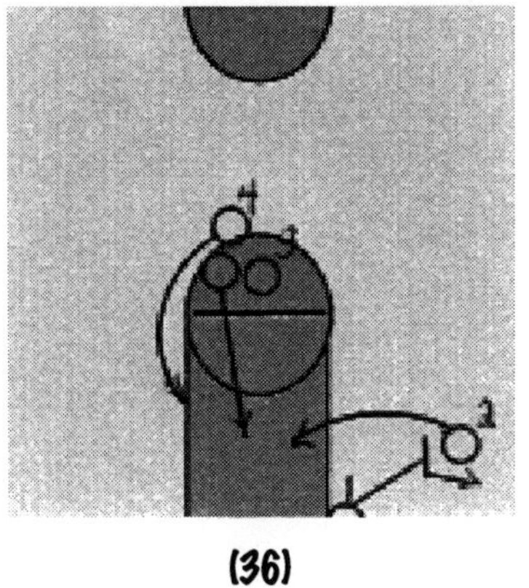

(36)

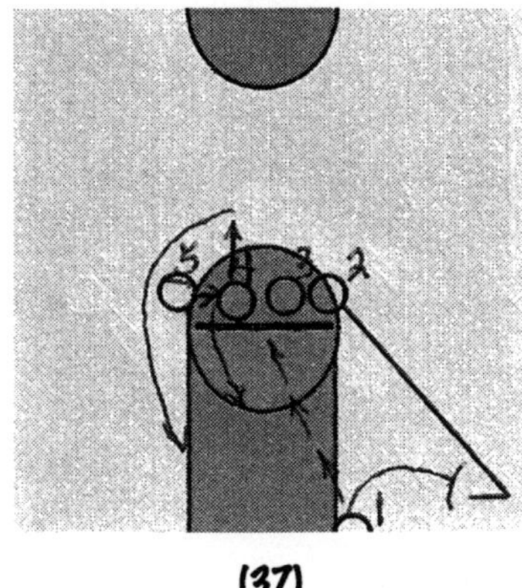

(37)

On a given signal, player 4 would pop out backwards toward the three-point line. Players 3 and 5 would slide tightly together; player 2 would sprint directly to the strong corner (where baseline and sideline connect). This would freeze player 2's man from interfering with the pass. A lob over the screen set by 3 and 5 would normally provide a high percentage set shot for player 4.

This is not our most desirable option. (See illustration #37.) We are first looking for cheaters, players that smell out and anticipate the play. For example, if player number 3's defensive player tries to disrupt the play by trying to steal the lob pass, that leaves player 3 wide open to the basket without a defender on him. Same is true for 5. If nothing develops but the lob to player 4, your inbounds play still has a strong variable to it. At this time, the players will somewhat be assembled in the above formation. Player 4 receives the ball and power dribbles to the right corner. This invariably calls his defender to follow and brings player 5's defender helping for a few steps. Player 4 now has the option to drive, which will be minimal; he will have a quick look at his teammate, player 5, who will cut directly to the basket and behind his defender who has been distracted toward the driver. He will also have the option of hitting player 2 after the following occurs: Player 3 will replace player 5's position. Immediately after the toss in to player 4 from player 1, player 1 sprints out to set a pick on player 2's defender. O2 reads the pick and flashes to the basket. O1 does not roll from the pick but holds firm for the three-point shot. Player 4 should be your point guard. Players 3 and 5 should be tall players. Obviously, player 1 should be your best three-point shooter.

I am always uncomfortable setting up a play that has designated players for designated positions. Once substituting has started, the success rate for these plays diminish due to the confusion of new positions and their roles.

I recognize that designated players, before substitutions, make these types of plays most successful. Perhaps they are valid plays, but it always seemed to me that it was like throwing dice—too much a gamble.

(Any variations of screening the screeners or involving the tosser in on the play are tactics to consider. I mention the previous five because they were time-tested, simple, and worked for our teams.)

A few gimmick inbounds plays:

1. Ten seconds to go in the game, and you have a comfortable lead. Call a time-out, talk for a second, ho-hum stuff. Then have your players break to the inbounds area. In a tight, tight, really tight side-by-side line with their toes nudging the sideline, have them hold their hands out directly in front of their chests. You now have eight eager hands outside the playing area asking for the ball. No one can post in front of or between your receivers. All the defenders will be behind your players. Hand the ball in, and have your players hand it back and forth from the end sideline tandem to the opposite end. Players must watch their balance so they don't get shoved out-of-bounds with the ball. No one player should hold it for over four seconds if you are in the front court lest the closely guarded rule would go into effect. Interesting idea: coaching your players to straighten their elbows when protecting the ball.
2. On an inbounds pass under the basket, some coaches do not defend the player tossing in the ball. Coach the tosser to watch for this and to take advantage of the tush of an opponent whose eyes are turned away. A sharp bounce off those cheeks and the tosser has a butt assist from the opponent for an easy lay in. Immediately following the made basket, a high-five with that opponent is cool, acceptable, and appropriate. Slapping the opponent's butt would not be appropriate.
3. First used by a high school in Portland, Oregon—the Barking Dog play. This is an inbounds play at the end court that needs a drama class student to help execute. Your drama student goes to the far corner of the court and

gets on his hands and knees. Your other players need to hover around randomly under the basket. Your hands-and-knees player now starts barking and howling very loudly in the direction of the upper seats. Have one of your players streak out to midcourt trying for the attention of the far referee, and have that player point at the barking dog. Those players in the free-throw area should all be pointing, laughing, and jockeying for viewing position of the dog. All but one, who—during this chaos—is going to receive a quick pass for a lay in. If it does not work, call it intermission or tell everyone that it was your assistant's idea.

4. Surely your referees all have a sense of humor? On administering the sideline pass during a dead ball, have your player who is throwing the ball in go up a few bleacher rows to throw it in. The rule book reads that a player can go as deep as he wants on the sideline, but not the end court.
5. Waste a Time-out play. This under-the-basket gimmick inbounds play begins with the coach shouting out, "Ken, you throw it in!" Tom is under the basket, and the referee has already administered the play to happen by handing Tom the ball. This all has to happen within five seconds. Tom mimics the coach shouting, "Ken, here you take the ball!" Others on the team look at Ken and point towards Tom, a little Hollywood directing aide, with help directions. With that command, Tom places the ball in his outstretched hand in a nonthreatening gesture to hand it over. Looking confused, Ken comes running over to take the ball. As Ken nears the basket, Tom makes a hard quick pass to Ken for the lay-in. Before the play begins and Tom has been handed the ball, Tom instructs the referee that he wants a time-out called when the referee's count nears violation time.
6. "Easy in." Offensive low-post man sets up on the opposite side of the basket from his teammate who is throwing in the ball. All other offensive players post up on the three-point line, equally distant from each other. The low-post receiver turns his side to the tosser and offers a hand held high on the baseline side. The defender will overplay to the post's extended arm to stop the lob pass. Once that pressure is felt by the offensive-post man, he needs to hook the defender with the same extended arm and pivot to that side of the defender toward the tosser. Pinning the defender behind his back and spinning to receive a bounce pass, he should be open. Any time the coaches used the phrase "run it again," that was our code for run the option to the last play. I think that any success that we experienced on this

misdirection vocal ploy was probably in spite of the code, and the option was just warranted then. Inbounding to the proper receiver needs to be practiced and understood, You and the team need to be on the same page on who should receive and why. The why is most important, for it teaches your players to think about their decisions should the last pass be to your best ball handler, your best free-throw shooter, your player who is being guarded by a player in foul trouble, or your player who is being defended by a poor defender or to the coach's son. For inbounds plays to be successful, everyone should be of common thought; it cannot be merely instructed. Like in anything else, the more you practice it, the better chance it has of becoming second nature rather than a time-using thought process.

Footwork Gimmickry

Two methods of free-throw footwork to use when your teammate is shooting:

1. The offensive player with the middle position on the free-throw line and close to the block should use a quick step in front of the low opponent; because he is low does not give him an automatic right to the screen out. At the least, your foot will collide with his nullifying his ability to step in front of you.
2. In the same position as above; however, you position yourself as far from the block as your short allocated position on the free-throw line permits. This will cause the low man to leave his position and distance himself from the basket to get his body on yours for a successful screen. This facilitates you for wrapping your inside hand around your opponent's waist and swinging him in the direction of his movement. In that motion, you swim over the opponent with your opposite outside hand, and presto, you now have the inside screen-out position. Our players were coached to alternate using these two moves. They were instructed to use no other movement. We felt the inside success from these two moves was consistent when played correctly, thus we accepted no excuses from our players for not complying. While speaking about free-throw lane positions, we asked our players to stay in them on a made shot. We wanted them to refrain from slapping the shooter's hand. I always felt that was a no-no. Why change or hurt the kinesthetic feeling of the shooter's recent successful touch? On a missed shot, just the opposite was recommended.

Screening Gimmicks

When you are defending an opponent that is setting a perimeter screen, you should show switch for anticipating the charge by the dribbler, but only show enough body to deter his driving while keeping your inside hand on the backside shoulder of the screener to hinder his smooth roll off his pick. If you're quick enough with good position, jump the screen for the charge. This has to be a high-percentage decision because you are leaving your man open.

Setting the down screen for the options of cutting, curling, and flaring, your teammate should grab your waist and pivot your body while executing one of three moves. By grabbing your teammate's waist, you stop the defender from fighting through the screen. If the low-post defender follows your post teammate around your screen, then your post should continue to curl around with the defender now in a following defensive position. If the defender cheats and fronts the screen, the post man back-cuts to the basket. If the defender plays behind the screen, the post needs to flare out toward the corner of the court for the short opener.

Mystery inbounds play—My son, who is a high school basketball coach, sheepishly recommended this play to me. He said, "Try it in practice. I don't know why it works, but it does." It is a goofy-looking play, one that seems more addled than confused. To lighten up a practice, I tried this carousel of a play. I huddled my offense together and explained the simplicity of its movement. The defense did not know what was coming. My offensive players posted up on the four corners of the key. Defense was man-to-man. Staying equally distant from each other, the offense began circling the key on the run. Two times in a row, the offense made simple uncontested lay ins. The third attempt, I improvised and had them run the opposite direction. Bingo! Another simple lay in. It works. It's hilarious. I never built my nerve up enough to run it in a varsity game. My junior varsity coach used it often and swore by it.

Simple Gimmicks

1. Use nicknames in practice. At game time, it is an advantage to use these sobriquets on the floor, without the opponents recognizing who you are addressing.

2. When you have lost your dribble in the backcourt, toss or shoot the ball against the backboard, secure the rebound, and you have reestablished dribble possession. Don't bounce it off the referee; you will double your problems.
3. It is important to practice a few offensive stalls. You may rather hire a lap dance from a nun than slow down the game of basketball, but there are times when sitting on the ball is comfortable and practical. Let's look at a few. Imagine you are nearing a two-possession game. In other words, the clock is running down and you have possession. The game is tied. There is no sense to hurry and score a two-point basket in time to deliver the opponent the ball for time enough to get a good look at a three-point shot. Doesn't that make sense?

Imagine another situation: Your lead and your opponent is packing the paint, and you are attempting to spread them or to bring them out. It would be sensible to do so with a structured team stall rather than your best dribbler playing keep-away and confusing his teammates as to his next action.

Let's imagine another situation, one where two or three of your regular starters have fallen into foul trouble before halftime and you need to bench them to protect them for reentering in the second half. Possibly your substitutes for these benched players are not blessed with shooting touch.

It would be remiss, in a situation like this, to not have a stall or semistall. To do differently and attempt to vie to keep the score as is while your starters are out might allow the opponents to amass an uncatchable lead or swing of momentum.

Our coaching staff was harmonious about removing a player from the game once he picked up his second foul in the first half. This was a hard rule to abide. It always felt like self-abuse; however, none of our coaching staff has ever seen a basketball game won in the first half. It has always paid off for us to have a full-strength team in the second half. We are not going to fall behind without our leaders on the floor. This tactical move of slowing down the game nullifies the opponent's matchup advantages. Trying to keep down their possessions and their offensive looks at the basket is crucial.

As a teacher, my number one goal was to set a motivational classroom for instilling, not facts and numbers, but *learning for the love of learning.* On the basketball floor, I looked for those players who were there for the intrinsic awards that come with the *love of practicing.* I advise you to seek those players who are passionately immersed in the wonderland of ball and basket. They are recognizable by their costumes, their individual focused practices, and their time devoted to improvement. A bonus is finding those players that are also leaders and encouragers. What have you done today to help improve a team player? Players that can answer that question are, affirmably, keepers.

I hope that this book of basketball plays, tricks, and gimmicks somewhat supplemented your knowledge and interest for the game of basketball. It is a challenging sport to participate in; when played by accomplished athletes, a beautiful, almost hypnotic, game to watch. I am preaching to the choir . . . Furthermore, I think high school and college basketball season-ending tournaments epitomize everything good about athletics. The most visual, the NCAA's, portray amateur athletes engrossed in pursuit of schoolroom success and court success. Their unbridled supporters, loud nonstop-playing bands, cheerleaders and song leaders, battling mascots, and avid fans do not shy from showing their unabashed devotion to their schools. Television news sprinkled with highlight collages of the contests, their color pageantry, and their scores seems to embrace even the nonseasonal fans. The excitement is contagious; every fan in every state in the nation shows involved devotion-toting bracket sheets for following the tournament outcomes. Unlike professional basketball that solicits the hype of various medias[*]. College March Madness needs no outside flavoring. To be a part of this diversion on an emotional level is enough; to be intimately involved as a coach, one should be so honored.

---

* September 5, 1979 - The NBA became a suspect marketing event when the Indiana Pacers signed Ann Meyers, a former UCLA Bruin, to an NBA contract.

Team Goals

This pyramid of success must begin with a good base. That good base is establish by your personal wants and needs. It is underwritten by your zest for excellence and commitment to work. You are going to be as good as you are willing to motivate your-self.

W—Non-structured school activities. (Your willingness to practice on your own. This is where your individual moves and skills are explored) Coaches do not make great players, players make great players.

O—Structured activities (Your willingness to be coached and advised) This is where your abilities are honed and meshed with other teammates to exploit the best of each as one.

L—Dressing, eating and drinking sensibly. making responsible decisions (refer to the team manual contract that you sign yearly) Demonstrate maximum effort in the classroom. Show your evidence of team before yourself. Always be willing to bring out the best in your teammates.

V—During season stay organized, keep up on your activities so one does not interfere with another. Be scientific regards your shot. Never leave the court on a missed shot. Shoot it over but not the same way you did when you missed.

E—'Prepare—Work—Execute' Analyze your own personal statistics weekly. Be analytical, don't slough off bad statistics to being in a slump. Work on the mechanics of those errors.

R—Set indicators to achieve personal and team goals.

I—Concentrate on summer work. Utilize those open gym dates.

N—Health and eligibility should be a common priority along with skills improvement.

E—Plan and prepare for this new season play as more than a bonus period but as a new chance to excel.

S—Put it all together!

1996 Captains: Cedra, Betsy & Fiona

Name____________________________ Date______________________

Pre-Game Exam

1. *We must play at ________________________ level in games and practices. (our highest)*
2. *Develop your ____________________for playing at maximum speed. (skills)*
3. *Playing at maximum speed is ________________________ to opponents.* (challenging)
4. *Basically the game of winning basketball equals__________ and_________. (T.O.'s & Fouls)*
6. *Practicing correctly and _________________ is what is needed to create (repetitively) carry-over to the game.*
7. *Games are won in the _______________half. (second half)*
8. *To create the type of pressure that involves little reaction time calls for _______________________. (playing quick)*
9. *Once you become a member of a team you must be willing to___________ (forfeit) your________________ rights. (individual)*
11. *Within our system fouls and________________ contribute the most to losing. (turnovers)*
12. *Rebounding involves interfering with the opponents path, keeping your arms high and_________________ the careen. (predicting) or reading*
13. *The fast break allows us:*
    a. *to exploit our speed and conditioning.*
    b. *to create the game tempo.*
    c. *to facilitate our complimenting______________s. (presses)*

14. *On offense we use three cuts for getting open. The _________ cut, the (V) 'L' cut with the arm over and the ________________. (pivot & bump)*
16. *On a down screen the post needs to grab the _________ of his teammate and (waist) then read.*
17. *What is the option to the inbounds 'cube' play? (cube again) or a better read*
18. *What is the importance to the post player holding his position until the down screener gets to him? (ideal transfer) location*
19. *Explain the differences between the cut, curl and flare off of a down screen.*

This questions answers must be demonstrated to a coach-have one sign off for you.

20. *The three important reasons for using the backboard shot is: (over shot advantage)*

    1._________________________(less demand

    2._________________________ on depth perception)

    3._________________________(advantage knowing careen)

23. *True or False The text book reason for the pick and roll is to create a (true) two on one situation.*
24. *What is the coverage of the defender in the open-trap when he is two passes away? (help position, center field)*

Pick up your test results in Coach Coste's office before school tomorrow morning.

Blanchet Boys' Basketball

Welcome to the Blanchet High School Boys' Basketball program. It is our desire, as a coaching staff, to help create a positive and successful experience for you as a Cavalier team member. To do this, we are concerned with the development of the whole individual, not just the part of you that is an athlete. It is our intent to provide opportunities which will develop character and strengthen values. We hope you learn more about life in general from being a member of this program. Suffice it to say, these ideals can only be realized if you, as a person, are totally committed to being a positive, sharing, and contributing member to this team.

We are looking for individuals who are devoted to their responsibilities as athletes and students; individuals who show desire and dedication on and off the floor. We are looking for athletes who are disciplined enough to maintain top physical condition throughout the season, and people who understand the importance of unselfishness and on-the-court cohesiveness. In short we are looking for winners. We, the coaches, are committed to giving our best, and thus we expect the same from you.

Team Expectations

Academic:

It is your responsibility as a member of this team, for yourself and for the team, to maintain good academic standing.

1. *We expect our team to maintain a combined 3.0 GPA average throughout the season.*
2. We also expect our players to show academic improvement each and every term.

Practice:

Practice determines success. It is in our practices that we develop the confidence, habits and skills, that are necessary for successfully carrying over into our games. Therefore, as we strive to be the best we can be, we must demand 100% effort in all that we do.

We as coaches expect:

1. for you to prepare yourself mentally for practice as you would for a contest.
2. that you will always have a specific goal for the day.
3. you to enter the gym under the auspices that no one is going to work harder than you do.
4. you to treat the practice floor as our classroom, we expect you to do non related socializing elsewhere.
5. you to use your pre-practice time wisely by working on your weaknesses and strengths.
6. when a coach is talking, that you look at them and listen to what they are saying. Don't justify your actions by telling a coach why you didn't accomplish a task, just get the job done.
7. when you are tired, to continue to be visible and encouraging.
8. hustle, clapping in to the huddles in and between drills; as we will do in the games.
9. you to be cocky in your play, don't confuse with over confident.
10. you to do something each practice to bring out the best in a teammate.

Practice punctuality:

Be on time and in your proper practice gear, in fact be early. Notify the coach as early as possible regards in expected tardiness or absence.

Excused absences:

One missed practice, during the week of a game disallows starting in the impending contest.

Two missed practices, during the week of a game, disallows participation in the impending contest.

Unexcused absences:

Two weeks team probation. Second violation is dismissal.

Injuries:

It is important that the coaching staff be made aware of injuries or illness prior to practice. If you are unable to practice but are able to be at practice, do so. You are still participating by your presence. It is imperative that you deal with injuries immediately as they occur. Failure to do so can significantly increase the severity of your injury as well as extend the rehabilitation time. Rule of thumb; "If you don't know what to do, immediately ice it." Get a flu shot in October if you haven't already.

Nutrition:

You will not be able to maximally perform if you do not eat properly. Breakfast is the meal that replenishes and strengthens the body. You are what you eat. Drink lots of water and listen to your parents. Pre-game carbohydrates, i.e., in the form of potatoes rather than sugars are preferred.

Dress code:

Any time you are representing Blanchet High School, you need to dress appropriately. When you travel as a team on a school day we require you to be in slacks, collared shirt and tie. During workouts penalties are assigned for those who are not in proper practice attire. When leaving the gym tired and exhausted your resistance to illnesses is going to be low. So dress appropriately wearing gloves and a head covering.

Training rules:

Team members shall follow the rules on consumption of alcoholic beverages, smoking or the use of illegal drugs as outlined in the High School 'Substance Abuse Policy' In or out of school your behavior must be appropriate. Inappropriate behavior may result in team suspension or expulsion.

We encourage all students who are interested in playing basketball to try out. However, participation in try outs does not ensure you of a preferred position. The varsity personnel will be selected after the first week of practice. Here are relative points to consider:

1. Do not assume for any reason that you are automatically on one squad or another. That must be earned.
2. If you played basketball for the Cavaliers last year that earns you nothing. You still must earn a spot on the team again.
3. If you are a senior, you must earn a spot on the varsity team. If you do not, then you must play on the junior varsity team, and any games must be pre-approved, because of your senior standing, for each contest by the opposition's coach.

There are pride and privileges associated with being a member of our team, one which you must continually earn the right to enjoy. This means taking care of business in the classroom, on the gym floor and at home. If in the course of the season we feel that a player should be moved from one team to another team, for the benefit of those teams or the player, we will move the player. As representatives of Blanchet High School, all team members are expected to conduct themselves in a manner consistent with a first class basketball program. We expect our players to show pride and commitment by completing all jobs, tasks and responsibilities given to them by their coaches, teachers and parents.

Your signature below acknowledges that you have read, understand and agree to comply with the expectations described in this team handbook. Good luck this season. "On to state!"

Players signature ______________________ Date____________________

Parent/Guardian signature ______________ Date____________________

30 October 2001

Dear Parents,

As a special friend of Cavalier athletics, I take this opportunity to personally invite you to follow Cavalier basketball this year.

It would be preferable to send personal notes but of course time does not permit it. Suffice it to say, we appreciate your help and support.

Please find enclosed a copy of our game schedule, the season's practice schedule, the Las Vegas Tourney itinerary, our player contract pamphlet which covers our philosophy statement, goals, expectations, rules and consequences, training and nutritional information, expectations and more.

You are encouraged to attend our practices as often as your personal schedules allow. You might focus early attention to our Blue-Gray inter-squad game where we can meet personally and discuss matters relative to the basketball program. That game is scheduled for 25 November at 6:00 pm.

Again, we the coaches thank you for your support and encourage you to follow us this year. We have a large turnout of players.

This turnout will support three strong squads, a varsity, junior varsity and freshman team, thus we have the highest expectations for this season.

"On to State!"

Sincerely yours,

William J. Coste
Head Basketball Coach
Blanchet High School

TOURNEY JOURNEY

November Practice Schedule

(Schedule of first presentation)

Monday	Tuesday	Wednesday	Thursday	Friday	Saturday
4 First Legal Practice Date - M/M Shell Help & Recover Match-Up	5 Free throws Ball side cut Give & Go Pick & Roll Free Thr Brk	6 Zone Traps Open Trap Drop Step Deny the Pass	7 Zone Defs: 131 H & S 32 & Jump Elbow Pass Dribble Pass	8 Zone Presses 1-2-1-1 1-3-1 2-2-1	9 Optional Open Gym
This weeks practice time is contingent on the Volleyball Team's advancement to State. If they are successfull practices will be at 7 or 7:30. If they fail to advance practices will be at 5:30pm all November.					
11 No School Vets Day Practice Time TBA	12 Early Off Zone Off	13 M/M Offenses Rebounding	14 Parent Teacher Conferences Practice Times TBA	15	16 Optional Open Gym
18 Blue White Games Team Mtg w/Parents	19 Needs	20 Needs	21 Thanksgiving	22 Needs	23 Optional Open Gym
25 **Girls Jamboree**	26 Needs	27 Needs	28 Needs	29 Needs	30 Optional Open Gym

Note: Next month practices for Varsity start after school each day
J.V.s start immediately following the boys varsity (Prox. 7:30pm)

Below is the coming year's basketball schedule. The reader will note that there are 12 league games scheduled and 10 non league encounters. All of the non league games are with 2-A schools or larger. Knappa was in the 2-A State Tourney last year. Jefferson as of late has had competitive teams. The two Seattle teams are both 3-A. We open their tournament against East Catholic High, last years league champion. They are regarded as State contender for this upcoming season. Little is known about Vernonia and the three Neah-Kah-Nie entries. Whatever the competition we always feel confident about the showing of our Alsea Lady Wolverines. We know they will be striving to complete their next years Team Goal: "To win the last game of the season!!!"

1997-98 Season Schedule

Date	Opponent	Site	Time Var
November 24, 1997	Jamboree	Alsea	TBA
December 1, 1997	Jefferson	There	7:00 P.M.
December 5, 1997	Perrydale	There	4:00 P.M.
December 9, 1997	Falls City	There	7:00 P.M.
December 12, 1997	Neah-Kah-Nie	There	TBA
December 13, 1997	Neah-Kah-Nie	There	TBA
December 16, 1997	Blanchet	There	5:30 P.M.
December 19, 1997	Triangle Lake	Alsea	5:30 P.M.
December 26, 1997	Holy Names	There	TBA
December 28, 1997	Holy Names	There	TBA
December 29, 1997	Alsea Tourney	Alsea	TBA
December 30, 1997	Alsea Tourney	Alsea	TBA
January 6, 1998	Vernonia	Alsea	5:30 P.M.
January 9, 1998	Eddyville	There	5:30 P.M.
January 10, 1998	Australian All-Stars	Alsea	TBA
January 13, 1998	O.S.D.	There	5:30 P.M.
January 17, 1998	Knappa	There	4:30 P.M.
January 20, 1998	Perrydale	Alsea	5:30 P.M.
January 23, 1998	Falls City	Alsea	5:30 P.M.
January 30, 1998	Blanchet	Alsea	5:30 P.M.
February 3, 1998	Triangle Lake	There	5:30 P.M.
February 10, 1998	Eddyville	Alsea	5:30 P.M.

1996-1997 Alsea Basketball

"Tourney Journey"

1998-1999 Alsea Basketball

"End of the Trail, Baker City"

Welcome to the Home Site of Alsea's Girl's Basketball team. Alsea is located in Oregon, 25 miles West of Corvallis on Hwy 34. Alsea is a small town of 500 citizens, but their girls basketball team is one of the best in the state. Through this current year of 1997, the Alsea girl's basketball teams have won the Southern Casco League championship every year of Coach Coste's tenure -since 1988- with the exception of 1992. Please come inside and look around. See the statistics from previous years, player information, team and player records, as well as statistics from this year.

Medical Consent and Release of Liability Form

We the undersigned parents or guardians, hereby grant permission for our son(s), ______________________ to participate in the Blanchet Boys' Basketball Camp. In consideration of being permitted to use the facilities, I hereby release said Blanchet Catholic School and its trustees, administrators, and employees from any and all liability for any damage or injury that any participant or my daughter may receive while on the premises of said school, both as to any right of action that may accrue to myself, my heirs and personal representative. This release includes all claims, demands, rights and causes of whatsoever kind of nature, arising from, and by reason of, any and all known and unknown, foreseen and unforeseen bodily and personal injuries, damage to property and the consequences thereof, that hereafter may be sustained.

It is further understood and agreed that I hereby authorize, **BLANCHET BOYS' BASKETBALL CAMP** also known as "Snappin' Twine" and its employees to secure the necessary services for my child in the event of an accident or illness. Further, I will be solely responsible for the payment of those services.

____

Parent/Guardian Signature **Date**

The participant has liability insurance with:

____

Policy # ______________________________

Family Doctor: ______________________

Dr. Phone #: ______________________

Does the player wear contacts?	Yes	No
Is the player allergic to bee stings?	Yes	No

List other allergies:

Include a list of any pertinent physical conditions:

Blanchet Cavalier

"Snappin' Twine" Camp

with

Wm. J. Coste

1999 National HS Basketball Coach of the Year

Boys only

High School Age
June 26 - 28

Mid-high & High School Age
July 3, 5 & 6
July 31 - August 2

Elementary School Age
August 5 - 7

Camp Highlights

- 3 pt. Contests
- Personal Critique Feedback Forms
- Most Improved Certificates
- Tournament Contests
- All-Star Team Game
- 3 on 3 Contests
- Hustle Awards
- Camp Store

Instructors

Wm. J. Coste

Blanchet High School Coach
1998 Oregon Coach of the Year
1998 Western States Coach of the Year
1999 National Coach of the Year

Bill Wold

MVP Far West Basketball Classic
Past Crescent Valley HW Head Coach
Past LBCC Head Basketball Coach

Todd Moore

Blanchet Asst. Varsity Coach

Bob Angove

Blanchet JV Basketball Coach

Camp will be held on the campus of Blanchet Catholic School.
4373 Market St. NE, Salem, OR 97301
HS Session - 2 p.m. - 7 p.m.
MH & HS Session - 9:30 - 2:30 p.m.
Elementary Session (grades 3-6) -1 p.m. - 4 p.m.

Cost per session: $50

The camp format is designed to develop skills therefore the primary focus will revolve around repetitive drills. Character building and team concepts will be stressed. Video playbacks and video highlights will be shared with the players as a further teaching tool.

Please enclose your check, made payable to *Blanchet Catholic School,* and send the following information to Wm. J. Coste at Blanchet Catholic School, 4373 Market St. NE, Salem, OR 97301

I wish to participate in the Blanchet "Snappin' Twine" Basketball Camp on ________________.
(date)

Name(s) ________________________________

Age(s) ________________________________

Phone No. ________________________________

Snappin' Twine Clinic

featuring OSU's **Ritchie McKay**

Date: October 13, 2000 (No school - State wide in service day)
Site: Blanchet HS - 4373 Market St. NE Salem, Or 97301
For: HS & Middle school coaches and general public
Info: Coach Bill Coste 503-391-2639

Times:	**Speakers**	**Topic**
9:00am	**Tom Kelly** Western Oregon Univ.	Running Game
9:45am	**Larry Doty** Linfield College	Basketball Essentials
10:30am	**Gordie James** Willamette University	Multiple Offensive Attack
11:15am	**Fred Litzenberger** University of Oregon	Oregon Defense
Noon	Host Lunch (For preregistered only) **Tom Welter,** O.S.A.A.	Hero Sandwiches Questions & Answers
12:30pm	**Ritchie McKay** Oregon State University.	To be Announced
1:15pm	**Joel Sobotka** Portland State University	Off. Opportunities for the 3 pt shot
2:00pm	**Rob Chavez** Univ. of Portland	Competitive Drills
2:45pm	**Bill Coste** Blanchet	Soft Presses

Cost: $50 If you preregister by Oct. 1, your lunch will be provided free.

****

Name______________________________ School____________________ List other attendee names on reverse side. Check enclosed for $____________ Make checks payable to Blanchet HS. **!!Door Prizes!**Vendors Available **!!Free coaches notebooks!!**A coaches placement board and opening game dates board will be available.

Blanchet Basketball

____________ Season Follow-Up

Name ______________________________ Date __________________

What personal goals for the 2008 season did you accomplish?w

____

____

What personal goals did you not accomplish? ______________________

Do you plan on pursuing those goals? ____________________________

What new goals do you have for yourself next year? ___________________

____

Do you see yourself as a starter? ________ At what position?______________

List what you feel are your strong points. __________________________

____

List what you feel are your weak points. ___________________________

____

Do these agree, with what you received from the coaches, in their end-of-the-year evaluation form? ____________________ Be frank.

List the weak parts of your game that the coaches recommended you work on.

____

What was your ending winter GPA? ____________

What are your short-term and long-term goals for academics; include this year.

____

____

Have your career plans changed? If so, to what? _____________________

____

Are you currently on a weightlifting program?_______ Be advised that

Do you plan on pursuing basketball at the collegiate level?_______________

Tell us something about yourself that we don't know. ?___________________

____

Coach Angove is opening the school weight room every Mon.-Wed.-Fri. at 5 p.m. This will continue through the summer. Also be advised that the gym will be open every Monday and Wednesday evening for free play at 5:30 p.m.

Do you plan on playing in our summer basketball league at the 'Hoop?'_____

We begin playing other schools after May 28 and will end on the 15th of July. Be further advised that I will be conducting four Snappin' Twine Camps for the Salem community. I hope to see you at one. If you wish individual instruction on any part of your game, please call me.

Do not hesitate to ask, for I enjoy this type of coaching and you will benefit from it.

Yours in basketball,

Coach Wm. J. Coste
(541)486-4045

Edwards Brothers,Inc!
Thorofare, NJ 08086
09 September, 2010
BA2010252